Parents and Virtues

Parents and Virtues

An Analysis of Moral Development and Parental Virtue

Sonya Charles

LEXINGTON BOOKS
Lanham • Boulder • New York • London

Published by Lexington Books
An imprint of The Rowman & Littlefield Publishing Group, Inc.
4501 Forbes Boulevard, Suite 200, Lanham, Maryland 20706
www.rowman.com

6 Tinworth Street, London SE11 5AL

British Library Cataloguing in Publication Information Available

Library of Congress Cataloging-in-Publication Data Available

ISBN 978-1-4985-5005-5 (hardback : alk. paper) | ISBN 9781498550079 (pbk : alk. paper)
ISBN 978-1-4985-5006-2 (electronic)

∞™ The paper used in this publication meets the minimum requirements of American National Standard for Information Sciences Permanence of Paper for Printed Library Materials, ANSI/NISO Z39.48-1992.

Printed in the United States of America

Contents

Acknowledgments

There are a number of people I would like to thank for helping me along this journey. I began this project during a professional leave semester supported by Cleveland State University. I also presented many of the chapters in this book at the Association for Practical and Professional Ethics national conference. The audiences there have given me encouragement and useful suggestions. I would like to thank my graduate school writing buddy Tricha Shivas for giving me feedback on an early chapter. I owe many thanks to friend and colleague Allison Wolf for reading multiple versions of many chapters—sometimes on a deadline! Her patient guidance has helped me to greatly improve many of the arguments presented here. Of course, any errors or missteps remain my own. I would also like to thank the anonymous reviewer of my draft manuscript for spotting some gaps in my arguments and providing helpful resources. Last, but not least, I owe a debt of gratitude to my husband and son who continue to give me encouragement and support.

Introduction

What Can Virtue Theory Tell Us about Parenting?

If we consider the responsibilities of parenthood, I think we should be struck by the enormity of this undertaking. Through the process of raising a child, parents are confronted with a variety of decisions—big and small. When is my son old enough to go on a sleepover to a friend's house? Should I let my teenage daughter get a tattoo? Will an allowance teach my twins to be responsible with money? Is my daughter's school providing her the resources she needs to succeed? This is just a small sample of the variety of questions parents will face. Obviously, the specific questions and dilemmas faced by particular parents will depend on the child, the parents, and the circumstances in which they find themselves. For example, a question about whether a school is providing what a child needs to learn will be different for a black parent in an affluent neighborhood, a white parent with a kid in a low-income neighborhood, or a parent of a child with autism. Each of these parents wants to see their children succeed, but they will face different challenges on their way toward that goal. Even though individual parents face different issues, I believe most parents want their children to be good people who are happy in their adult lives. As such, a central motivating question of this book is how can parents raise a kid to be a moral and flourishing person?

At first glance, we might think this question is better left to psychologists rather than philosophers. It is true that if you consider the traditional ethical theories found in philosophy, they do not seem to address these issues. Since they focus on the decisions and actions of adults, most have little to say about children, let alone parenting them. I propose that Aristotle's ethical theory (known as virtue theory) is an exception. Aristotle asks how do we become a moral person and how does that relate to leading a good life? In other words, his motivating questions are very similar to goals parents have for their children.

For example, most parents want their children to be good people. But what is the best way to accomplish this goal? Aristotle would say that we should start by creating good habits under the guidance of a mentor. Consider how often parents remind children to say please and thank you. Parents are trying to create a habit of being polite. Similarly, if we want to teach children to be generous and kind, we may start by encouraging a young child to share her candy with a friend. Later, when the child earns an allowance, we may encourage her to give to a local charity. If we continue to encourage the child to practice these kinds of behaviors on a regular basis, she will develop a habit of giving/sharing—being kind.

However, simply participating in certain behaviors is not enough. As parents, we all recognize when children robotically say thank you or give an apology that is not sincere. While we cannot force children to have the appropriate emotions, we can hope they will come to understand why we do things like apologize, and eventually their behaviors will become more sincere. As we can see, the kinds of actions we are most interested in have both an affective or emotional component as well as a cognitive or rational component. If I always remember to offer you something to drink when you visit me, but I resent having to do this, then I am not really being a very gracious host. Indeed, if you consider us to be friends, but I am constantly (secretly) resentful toward you, then my actions may even be duplicitous. So, while Aristotle argued that creating habitual behaviors makes it *easier* to do the right thing, he recognized that moral development also requires that a person knows why she is doing a certain action and agrees with these reasons for her actions.

In this way, Aristotle recognized that moral development was a process. While it starts with performing certain actions that create habits, eventually we must also learn moral reasoning, which includes understanding the reasons for our actions. For Aristotle, this next step was the cultivation of practical wisdom, which included coming to a more nuanced understanding of the virtues and how to express them. For example, suppose you are teaching your child to be kind and generous. You are doing your job well and your son wants to buy his friend an elaborate birthday present. Your son could easily afford this present and knows it is something his friend would really enjoy. However, the friend does not have access to the same resources as your son and, while he may love to have this gift, he may also feel a bit intimidated or embarrassed. After all, this friend would never be able to reciprocate with a gift as elaborate as this one. In helping your child understand and navigate situations like this, you are helping him learn practical wisdom.

The ultimate goal is for your child to understand what it means to be a moral person, to adopt these values as his own, and to be able to make decisions based on these values for himself when presented with a new or novel situation. In this way, these values (or virtues) become what Aristotle calls a state-of-character. At this stage, a person has cultivated a tendency to do the right thing (habituation) and reasoning skills that allow him to know what the right thing to do is (practical wisdom). Most importantly, these values or virtues are identity constituting for him—they are part of who he is and/or integral to how he understands himself.

According to Aristotle, we should focus on developing our character—if we work on being virtuous in our daily life, then we will make moral decisions; we will be moral beings. The focus is not on whether we follow the right rules all (even some of) the time nor on whether someone believes the right things. Instead, it is about developing into a good person who acts for the right reasons, in the right ways, at the right times, and to achieve the rights sorts of goals. This is determined based on the context, and part of being virtuous is learning how to figure all of this out. I believe Aristotle's approach fits well with the way most people approach parenting. While we may give children some rules of thumb, we often focus more on character traits; we worry about the kind of kid we are raising. Are they honest? Trustworthy? Compassionate? Driven? Curious? The specifics will vary but I firmly believe that parents want to raise "good kids," however they define those terms. In other words, parents want to do the very thing Aristotle is trying to teach us.

Of course, Aristotle's theory is far from perfect and there are parts of it that require updating. Still, given the above, I think that a neo-Aristotelian virtue theory (one that avoids Aristotle's problems but still maintains its core ideas) has many advantages when assessing a variety of questions related to the ethics of parenthood. To show this, in this book I approach the ethics of parenthood in two different ways.

In part I, I consider what the basic components of Aristotelian virtue theory can tell us about the project of parenting. Even though Aristotle did not focus a lot of attention on the specifics of parenting, he does recognize the important role parents play in a child's life. In the first three chapters, I consider the parent-child relationship in relation to some major concepts or ideas from Aristotle's theory—instilling virtue, practical wisdom, and flourishing.

Chapter 1 takes a closer look at the process of moral development. Here I bring together psychological theories and empirical data on moral development and show how it relates to key aspects of Aristotle's theory—specifically, habituation, practical wisdom, and a state-of-character. The psychological literature supports much of Aristotle's theory. For example, the process of teaching children to empathize employs techniques that mirror Aristotle's understanding of habituation (e.g., practicing doing the right thing) and practical wisdom (i.e., a kind of moral discernment). Theories of moral development also help us understand how we come to develop our own morality or make things our own in what Aristotle would call a state-of-character.

While most of my discussion thus far has focused on children, Aristotle's concepts are also useful in thinking about parents. In Aristotle's theory we should all work to be virtuous, and the concepts outlined earlier apply to parents as well as children. In chapter 2, I consider what it means to have practical wisdom in the context of parenting. For Aristotle, practical wisdom comes from experience. It is a mix of practical and ethical knowledge that allows one to get things right. What does it mean to be a practically wise parent? Much of it relates to getting to know your child. There are a variety of goals related to parenting, and a parent must think about how to best meet those goals. In making these decisions, the intimate knowledge one has about one's own child will be a key component in getting things right, but other kinds of knowledge may be useful as well.

For Aristotle, cultivating the virtues and living a virtuous life will help one to flourish—this is the end goal of virtue theory. Similarly, I believe most parents hope their children will flourish. However, as Aristotle noted, we need a society that supports citizens' ability to flourish, and, unfortunately, not all children have an equal opportunity to flourish in our current society. Chapter 3 addresses the issue of systemic injustice and how it undermines flourishing for some groups. I consider not only how parents attempt to deal with injustice, but also why it requires revisions to Aristotle's theory.

After considering what key aspects of Aristotle's theory can tell us about the general goals of parenting, I realized that virtue theory might also be helpful in analyzing specific questions. In part II of the book, I shift my focus to consider some issues that present potential moral dilemmas for parents and whether there are specific parental virtues we may want to use to guide parental actions. One of my main areas of research is bioethics, and the questions I take up in the second half of the book grow out of bioethical debates. Bioethicists rarely draw on virtue ethics when analyzing moral dilemmas. I believe this is because virtue ethics is seen as less action-guiding than other traditional ethical theories such as deontology or utilitarianism. Building on the work of Rosalind Hursthouse and Rosalind McDougall, I hope to show this is a mistaken assumption. In each chapter, I show how a virtue theory approach can help us analyze a particular question or issue. The scenarios discussed in these chapters help to illustrate how virtue theory draws our attention to certain morally salient features. I also consider whether there are specific parental virtues that can help guide our actions.

Chapter 4 explores the virtue of trustworthiness and what it would say about the use of "donor" gametes in procreation. I had been studying the debates over whether children should have access to information about their genetic parents for years. While I had sympathy with the rights-based arguments, they seemed to miss other aspects of what I found so troubling about parents who chose to keep this information secret. Virtue theory and the idea of trustworthiness as a virtue helped me to resolve this dilemma. As I hope we will see, it has also proved useful for more fully assessing other debates in bioethics.

In chapter 5, I join the ethics of parenthood debate over the limits of parental autonomy in relation to children's rights. In bioethics, this is usually related to questions about choosing for or against certain traits in children and/or the ability of parents to make life-altering medical decisions for very small children. However, the kinds of questions raised by these issues can also lead to broader questions about the scope of parental authority and how far parents can go in shaping the child's future options (or lack thereof). In relation to these debates, I give a more detailed explanation of what I find problematic about a rights-based approach. I also begin to outline an alternative virtue theory approach using the virtue of acceptingness as well as the concepts of flourishing and (parental) practical wisdom.

Finally, in chapter 6, I consider the virtue of committedness and the decision to become a parent. Specifically, I look at cases where a person chooses to become a parent, but then either cannot or will not continue to be a parent until the child reaches maturity. The main cases I consider are those who choose to become a parent knowing they will likely die (either from age or illness) before the child reaches adulthood, or a person who chooses to have a child and then walks away from that responsibility. There are many responsibilities one takes on when deciding to become a parent. The main question I consider in this chapter is: When one invites a child into the parent-child relationship, what kind of commitment has one made?

In the end, I hope this project encourages others to think about how virtue ethics can be useful for both bioethics and debates in the ethics of parenthood literature. I also hope it reignites some conversations among virtue theory scholars. As we will see, there has been some debate over the nature of habituation and how the stages of moral development relate to Aristotle's theory. However, there are many other questions worthy of inquiry. I invite others to join me in exploring these issues.

Part I

The Parental Role in Upbringing

Chapter One

Instilling Virtue

The Process of Moral Development

Given the importance of a proper upbringing for Aristotle's theory of virtue, it is surprising that the particulars of moral development have not received more attention in virtue theory. This is not to say there has been no reflection on the course of moral development in relation to Aristotle's theory, but some parts of Aristotle's theory have received more attention than others. Also, I do not believe the role of parents has been given the kind of sustained attention it deserves. Building on this earlier work, I bring together theoretical analysis of Aristotle's main components of morality—habituation, state-of-character, and practical wisdom—with empirical research on moral development. While many things contribute to a specific child's moral development, my main focus is on the role of parents. Given what psychology tells us about moral development, how would a virtuous parent best facilitate this process?

HABITUATION

Aristotle argues that children need a good upbringing to develop virtue, and habituation is a key component of that upbringing. For our current purposes, there are three important aspects of habituation. First, the child must practice doing virtuous acts. Just as a builder or musician practices her craft, a child must practice virtuous behavior. However, we know that behavior is not enough for Aristotle. For an act to be truly virtuous, we must also have the correct corresponding feelings. So the second thing we must do is train the child's emotions to take pleasure in the right things. All children pursue pleasure. Habituation teaches children to find pleasure in being virtuous. This is perhaps the most controversial aspect and where I will focus the following discussion. Third, habituation requires a virtuous mentor (usually parents, teachers, etc.). Children do not yet reliably recognize what is virtuous so they need someone to help them identify virtuous acts. How the mentor guides children to recognize virtuous acts and take pleasure in virtuous things is also a matter of debate that I will address below.

How does habituation lead to virtue especially in the sense of training the emotions? As Jeannie Kerr summarizes, there are two main approaches to this question—the mechanical view and the cognitivist view. Much of this debate hinges on how we understand emotions. For those who support the mechanical view, there is more of a conceptual divide between feelings and thought.

> A key assumption in the mechanical view is that engaging in repeated experiences does not contain a cognitive dimension and thus habituation (as the repeated experience of guided moral action) is unlikely to result in the development of the excellences of character. . . . Implicit in the mechanical view is that a child's experience of acting virtuously does not provide for the possibility of the child having thoughts and feelings about the act itself. (Kerr 2011, 647)

Given that, in the mechanical view, thought plays little to no role in emotions, these theorists find Aristotle's move from doing to feeling more mysterious. To understand the problem, let's take a closer look at this theory.

In their article on habituation, Jan Steutel and Ben Spiecker explain what they call a "non-cognitive account" of Aristotle's theory. They are particularly interested in the connection between frequently performing virtuous acts and "the development of virtuous sentimental dispositions" (Steutel and Spiecker 2004, 537). In general, they see the doing of virtuous acts as good for developing skills or habits, but not for cultivating appropriate emotional responses: "habits are dispositions to *do* certain kinds of things, and not, for example, dispositions to be affected in certain ways under particular circumstances" (Emphasis in original. Steutel and Spiecker 2004, 539). Where Steutal and Spiccker do see the possibility for affective training is in the role of the tutor. However, even here the focus is on response to pleasurable and painful stimuli while ignoring any other possible cognitive aspects of the emotions.

> Given the fact that the tutor is a person with virtuous cares and concerns, we can sketch a more sophisticated picture of the role of pleasure and pain in habituating the child. As a reaction to the child's behaviour, the tutor will not merely give the child a reward when he is acting rightly, or confront him with unpleasant things when he is acting wrongly, but also show in word or deed all

kinds of feelings and emotions. If the child is acting as virtue requires, the tutor will respond with positive feelings and emotions, showing joy, delight, elation, relief or pride, and if the child is acting contrary to virtue, the tutor will exhibit negative feelings and emotions, such as distress, sorrow, anger, sadness or disappointment. (Steutel and Spiecker 2004, 545)

According to this theory, the child learns to take pleasure in virtue and pain in vice through an identification with the mentor/parent. There is no cognitive component to this response, just a behavioral response to reinforcement and punishment. In this way, theorists who adopt the mechanical view see habituation as a form of conditioning.

As we can see, this view has a hard time making sense of Aristotle's theory. Clearly, "habituation" implies developing a kind of habit; however, Aristotle wants more than mere conditioning. For Aristotle, our virtuous actions cannot be only a behavioral response, but must also include appropriate cognitive responses. Is the identification with a parent/mentor enough? I would argue that it is not. While a desire to please a parent/mentor may lead a child to work at cultivating virtuous habits, it is hard to see how this helps children develop skills they need to move from habituation to practical wisdom. One problem here is that the emotional connection is directed only toward the mentor. The focus is on pleasing the tutor versus learning to take pleasure in being virtuous for its own sake. This will require some cognitive components as the child gets a general sense of behaviors the mentor will find pleasing versus those that will bring punishment. However, this theory is non-cognitive in the sense that there is no reflection on the nature of the actions themselves. As we will see, the cognitive account is different in at least two ways—a richer understanding of the cognitive aspects of emotion and, consequently, an emphasis on cultivating the right thoughts and attitudes in relation to virtuous behaviors. For these reasons, I find the cognitivist theory a more compelling explanation of Aristotle's approach.

As the name implies, cognitivist theorists argue that feelings are imbued with thoughts; therefore, the transition from doing to being is smoother for them. For example, Kerr summarizes Nancy Sherman's view (which I will discuss in more detail below):

Sherman argues that virtuous action involves a series of steps, and that the action itself is preceded by the discriminating perception of a certain situation, including reactive emotions as part of that response, together with desires and beliefs about the situation. (Kerr 2011, 648)

A classic example (that is also discussed by Aristotle) is anger. Anger is a response to some slight or injustice, but to make this judgment, we must have some beliefs about how people should treat each other as well as beliefs about the intentions of the one at whom our anger is directed.[1] In this way, emotions are bound up with beliefs and judgments—they have a strong cognitive component.

As we might expect, the cognitivist theorists have a far different understanding of how habituation shapes affective responses necessary for virtue. Nancy Sherman argues that we need a conception of habituation that takes cognitive and affective development into account and also includes reflective and critical aspects. Drawing on Aristotle's analysis of the emotions in the *Rhetoric*, Sherman argues that his understanding of the emotions includes cognitive components. In thinking about how we can reform desires or train the affective aspects of self, Sherman states:

> I want to argue that Aristotle's explicit theory of emotion as intentional or cognitive provides us with a clue: emotions will be educated, in part, *through their constitutive beliefs and perceptions*. Cultivating the dispositional capacities to feel fear, anger, goodwill, compassion, or pity appropriately will be bound up with learning how to discern the circumstances that warrant these responses. Hitting the mean in our affective response, i.e., getting right the degree and nuance of the reaction, and in general its inflection, would be inconceivable apart from some critical judgement which informed it. (Emphasis added. Sherman 1989, 166–67)

Feelings include certain beliefs or judgments; they are about something. So, in learning to recognize situations that call for virtuous actions, children are also learning a kind of critical discernment. To recognize something as "that" kind of case is a critical activity that precedes deliberation and action.[2]

For Sherman, the process of habituation is much more complex and nuanced than the kind of conditioning proposed by Steutel and Spiecker. Habituation will include developmentally appropriate explanations that encourage inquiry and reflection. Rather than simply trying to curtail or enhance some emotions, the parent tries to shape the child's emotions so she sees the situation in the correct way. As Sherman puts it, "Education is thus a matter of bringing the child to more critical discriminations" (Sherman 1989, 172). Thus, this kind of improvement is focused on increasing the child's own internal skills of discernment.

If we consider the psychological work on moral development, we find that it also supports the cognitive view. For this discussion, I rely mainly on John Gibbs's *Moral Development and Reality*. In this work, Gibbs synthesizes two major theories of moral development—Lawrence Kohlberg (justice) and Martin Hoffman (empathy). For now, I focus on the development of empathy, but I will say a bit about the connection between justice and empathy later in the discussion of practical wisdom. Let me also offer a quick clarification about the relationship between empathy and virtue. While I believe the process of empathic moral development is very similar to the process of learning virtue, I am not prepared to argue that empathy, itself, is a virtue. Instead, I would argue that it is necessary for other virtues—such as beneficence and charity. My claim here is similar to Daniel Russell's argument that self-respect and virtue reinforce each other (i.e., they have a reciprocal relationship), but self-respect (alone) is not a virtue (Russell 2005). Let us now turn to the role of empathy in moral development.

Building on Hoffman's theory, Gibbs defines empathy as "a biologically and affectively based, cognitively mediated, and socialized predisposition to connect emotionally with others" (Gibbs 2003, 79). As we can see, proper empathy requires three related components: a biological basis, cognitive development, and socialization that helps facilitate internalization. According to Aristotle, when contemplating what counts as a virtue or how the virtues work, we need to start with the facts of human existence. In this case, we see that humans are born with biological responses that predispose us toward empathy. Specifically, the infant has biological responses that allow her both to interact affectively with others and to create affective associations with certain situations or events. Later in life, these biological responses continue; however, they become more sophisticated as we cognitively develop. Ultimately, Hoffman and Gibbs argue that we need a biological component for socialization to be successful, but for mature empathic responses, this biological component must be supplemented with a cognitive component (Gibbs 2003, 80).

In the moral development literature, we see that cultivating empathy starts as a form of habituation. When we are young, our egocentric desires often override our natural empathetic tendencies. For example, consider a preschool age child who really wants to play with a new toy. John snatches the toy from David and continues to play with it ignoring David's cries. Psychological research shows that in other situations John would likely notice and have empathy for David's distress. However, in this circumstance, his own egocentric desires lead him to ignore David's cries—his attention is diverted so the normal biological responses are subdued or extinguished. According to Hoffman, this is a teachable moment. If a parent intervenes and draws John's attention to (a) David's distress (which is likely to activate the biological component) and (b) his own role in causing that distress (which draws attention to the salient cognitive element that is currently being ignored), the parent can help draw out the appropriate empathetic responses. Hoffman calls these "inductions" and, if done correctly, they can play a pivotal role in cultivating the young child's empathic moral development.

However, these interventions need to be correctly implemented. As Hoffman explains, the interventions need to activate empathic responses. Specifically, Hoffman advocates the use of "inductions" or parental messages that "highlight the other's perspective, point up the other's distress, and make it clear that the child's action caused it" (Hoffman quoted in Gibbs 2003, 100). In other words, redirecting attention to the salient cognitive aspects helps to

activate the appropriate biological aspects.[3] By refocusing the child's attention to the salient features of the incident, the parent hopes to activate the
natural empathy tendencies that have been overridden due to the child's
current egocentric bias. Through these inductions, parents can help train a
child to focus his or her attention on the salient features of a situation. As we
get older and our cognitive development increases, our egocentrism will
naturally decline. The cognitive ability to consider multiple ideas and viewpoints helps lessen the natural pull of egocentrism (even though it will always remain to some degree). The combination of this continual refocusing
and the child's natural cognitive growth will eventually lead to more mature
empathic moral development.

We can see that this kind of training is very similar to Aristotle's conception of habituation. The parent is helping train the child in appropriate empathic responses that (hopefully) motivate him to do the right thing. This
process also lends more support to the cognitivist view of habituation than
the mechanical view. Consider this description of habituation by Sherman:
"The discrimination of ethical relevance will ground affective responses. By
tutoring the child's vision of the world, by instructing him to attend to these
features rather than those, desires become focused and controlled in specific
ways" (Sherman 1989, 169). In Gibbs's theory, we redirect the child's focus
to activate his empathic responses. What is important is that John caused
David's distress, not John's desire for and pleasure in the new toy. Also
notice how, if this redirection is successful, it makes the entire situation shift
for John. Previously his cognitive/affective awareness focused on his intention to get the toy and his enjoyment in playing with it. If we successfully
shift his cognitive/affective response to focus on how his actions harmed
David, then he will view his actions (and possibly himself) in a different
way.[4] The kaleidoscope has shifted and now John views the entire encounter
in another way.

In contrast, the mechanical view ignores these cognitive aspects of the
situation and instead emphasizes a kind of conditioning via pleasures and
pains.[5] Suppose instead of seeing this as a teachable moment, the parent or
teacher simply goes up to John and snatches the toy away from him and gives
it back to David. Along with this action, the parent chastises John and perhaps gives him further punishment in the form of a spanking or time-out.
What has John learned? He has learned to fear his parent or perhaps a lesson
about not getting caught. Without consideration of the cognitive components
of emotions, there is no training of the affect or critical discernment of the
situation. In sum, John is not learning to recognize the morally salient features of the situation.

In fact, we can see this even more clearly when we think of how upbringing can go wrong. Returning to the empirical research, Gibbs points out
specific cognitive distortions that undermine empathy and can lead to antiso-

cial behavior. If children are not trained to cultivate their empathic predispositions, they remain egocentric and this egocentrism can lead to cognitive distortions that effect moral judgment. For example, many antisocial youth blame others for their own antisocial behavior (e.g., "He made me do it," "She was asking for it."). Here we see why the relationship between the cognitive and the affective is so important. Without a proper understanding of the situation, a person will not have the correct emotive response (or react with the appropriate action). Gibbs explains this using what he calls veridical moral perception. I believe this parallels Sherman's conception of critical discernment. To better understand these concepts, I turn now to a discussion of how they continue to develop as the child gets older and, consequently, gains a more mature morality.

STATE-OF-CHARACTER

According to Aristotle, we cannot be fully virtuous if we simply follow an ingrained habit. To be truly virtuous, the virtue must also be a state-of-character. Rosalind Hursthouse addresses this aspect of moral development in *On Virtue Ethics*. Children might perform an act that is in accord with a specific virtue. They may even give you an acceptable reason for that action. But, according to Hursthouse, this action is still not fully virtuous because they do not yet have values of their own. Their characters are still forming. In this way, they cannot fully embody the virtue in question. As Hursthouse explains, "ascribing 'moral motivation,' 'because she thought it was right,' is ascribing something that goes far beyond the moment of action. It makes a claim about *what sort of person the agent is*—a claim that goes all the way down" (Emphasis added. Hursthouse 2001, 160). Here I briefly consider the kind of internalization necessary for something to be a "state-of-character."

Hoffman argues that for mature empathy-based morality, the child must eventually internalize the social norm—this is the goal of socialization (and this internalization shares a striking resemblance to our Aristotelian conception of a state-of-character).

> An internalized moral norm is one that has been *appropriated* or adopted as one's own. In other words, the child (a) experiences the normative information "as deriving autonomously from within oneself" (Hoffman, 2000, p. 135), (b) feels compelled by an inner obligation to live up to it even in the absence of witnesses or external reward and punishment, and (c) feels empathy-based transgression guilt and/or engages in reparative or other prosocial behavior toward the victim in the event of a failure to live up to the norm. (Gibbs 2003, 102)

Similar to Hursthouse's description, we see that internalized norms about appropriate empathic responses are self-motivating (i.e., they motivate the person to act virtuously) and cultivate the appropriate feelings toward a virtuous action (i.e., the person wants to do it because it is part of who he or she is, not because he or she seeks reward or avoids punishment). To translate this into Aristotelian language, a mature empathic morality motivates the person to act "from a fixed and permanent state" and, according to Hursthouse, this is required for a fully virtuous action (Hursthouse 2001, 135–36).

In order to further flesh out the relationship between moral development and Aristotle's conception of a state-of-character, I turn to Paul Benson's theory of normative competence.[6] Benson is primarily interested in explaining the nature of free action (not virtue theory), but the values component of his definition is useful for our current analysis. Benson considers the actions of a young child who breaks the rules to play on his desk. The child knows this is against the rules—indeed the danger of getting caught is part of the fun. Even though the girl's actions are fully intentional, Benson argues they are not fully free. Again, I am not interested in the debate over free action, but more so in Benson's conception of how values relate to this. He argues that the girl's actions cannot be fully free because she does not fully understand the evaluative concepts related to this behavior.

> Though the child deliberately plays on my desk without asking me, knowing that I really do not like her to do this, she is not mature enough to understand why I do not like her up on my desk or why this dislike, connected with the importance of a private work space, is reasonable. (Benson 1987, 476)

Specifically, she does not understand the broader importance of privacy, respecting others work, and so forth. So, while her specific *behaviors* may be inconsiderate or rude, we do not consider the child, herself, to be an inconsiderate or rude *person*.

Some may question whether we should even call her behaviors rude or inconsiderate given that she does not fully understand the norm. I think we can. As with many things in virtue theory, this is a continuum. Children begin with a fairly basic or rudimentary understanding of moral norms and, ideally, these become more sophisticated over time. Even very young children can have a general understanding of what it means to be rude. They simply do not understand the broader norms that support these practices. As such, they do understand the implications for a person's character.

In his theory, Benson draws a connection between normative competence and character development. The young girl's actions tell us *something* about her character—that she is willful or mischievous. Yet, we do not make the broader normative judgment that she is a *rude* person because we know she does not fully understand (and therefore cannot have internalized) the broader values (and corresponding virtues/vices) attached to her actions. I would argue this is why our reaction to a small child ruining our work because she was messing at our desk is qualitatively different from the reaction we would have to our spouse or roommate doing the same thing. We would expect an adult to have the appropriate normative competence and judge them accordingly. For this reason, Benson argues that free actions have the *potential* to tell us something about what *kind* of person the one performing the action is.

> Actions are fully our own when they may serve to express what we are like as persons, when they are potential vehicles of self-disclosure. That is, our free acts are suitable grounds on which certain sorts of evaluative appraisals of us may be formed. (Benson 1987, 481)

In other words, I would say free actions (on Benson's definition) tell us something about a person's state-of-character.

In fact, Benson's definition of normative competence seems to relate to both state-of-character and practical wisdom. He consistently argues that free actions are potential avenues of self-disclosure because they are related to our values. Specifically, Benson says, "one's action is fully free only to the extent that one has the ability to appreciate the normative standards governing one's conduct and to make competent critical evaluations, in light of those norms, of open courses of action" (Benson 1987, 475). In other words, a person needs the maturity and experience to understand the broader import of the values in play. This means the person needs to understand the status of certain values within the cultural context as well as how her actions will be interpreted in relation to those values. It is worth noting that Benson does not say we have to agree to or enact those values promoted by our culture, we simply need the normative competence to understand them and, thus, what our actions will say about us.

In sum, this tangent helps explain why small children are usually not presumed to have a state-of-character in the Aristotelian sense—namely, they do not have the necessary normative competence. Leaving out the free action portion, Benson's discussion nicely parallels the descriptions given by Hursthouse and Gibbs. We see now that, as Hursthouse says, children may give you reasons for their actions, but they do not have values of their own because they cannot fully understand those values. Since they do not have a full understanding of the values, they cannot internalize them in a way that makes them their own or, as Gibbs says, feel an inner obligation to live up to them. To clarify, by "full" understanding, I mean the ability to understand the broader implications we have been discussing as well as the self-disclosure aspects—that is how these specific behaviors fit into a broader moral framework and what our behaviors will say about us as a person. Indeed, I believe this broader understanding is part of the process of internalization. I shift from doing things to please my mentor and instead begin to do them because that is the kind of person I wish to be.

As I pointed out earlier, this discussion helps explain the interrelatedness of the three components of Aristotle's theory under discussion. We may habituate children to be considerate and polite, but, like the child playing on the desk, they cannot fully appreciate those virtues until they have a broader understanding of how social relations work. For instance, in the desk example, the child needs to understand the importance society puts on privacy, how the work reflects the time and mental energy the adult put into it, and so on. Similarly, the virtues of being considerate and polite also entail an understanding of taboo topics of conversation and who justly (or unjustly) deserves respect. Without this kind of practical wisdom, the child cannot properly internalize the virtue or be motivated by it. In other words it cannot be considered a state-of-character. As always, this will be an ongoing process that admits of degrees. Indeed, Aristotle viewed the process of living virtuously as a lifelong endeavor. My main point here is simply to give some explanation of an important developmental shift. This discussion also highlights skills necessary for both practical wisdom and a state-of-character.

We again see how the cognitive theory fits better with our empirical and theoretical understanding. If habituation is primarily a form of conditioning through pleasure and pain, then the child is not learning the skills of discernment necessary to properly internalize the values or, later, develop practical wisdom. According to Howard Curzer, another mechanical theorist, habituation simply teaches which acts are right or wrong and the learning of why acts are right or wrong comes later (Curzer 2002). It is true that the learning of why acts are right or wrong comes later. However, the problem with the mechanical view is that it neglects the teaching of *skills* that will be necessary to understand the why. Aristotle recognized this as well. In the *Nicomachean Ethics*, he claims that for teaching and argument to be effective "the soul of the student must first have been cultivated by means of habits for noble joy and noble hatred, like earth which is to nourish the seed" (1179b24–26). An overly simplistic explanation of what Aristotle means by "noble" would include some broader understanding of why the virtue is a virtue.[7] As we have seen, this is part of the understanding necessary for normative competence or a state-of-character. I would argue that the discernment discussed by Sherman and the inductions discussed by Gibbs are one way to begin cultivating the cognitive skills that will be necessary for developing this kind of understanding that is necessary for a virtuous state-of-character and practical wisdom.

PRACTICAL WISDOM

Now I take a closer look at the relationship between the affective and cognitive components of mature empathy. We saw from our earlier discussion that empathy includes biological, affective, and cognitive components.[8] We should notice right from the beginning how well this blends with a neo-Aristotelian understanding of the virtues. As Hursthouse explains, an Aristotelian understanding of virtue occupies a kind of middle ground that blends reason and the passions or inclinations, and, to be fully virtuous, these must be aligned in the right way. Habituation trains the emotions and desires toward virtuous actions. Hopefully, these responses are eventually internalized, thereby creating a virtuous state-of-character. Finally, we must refine our skills of discernment and deliberation in order to have practical wisdom. I turn now to a discussion of what sort of knowledge and experience is important for developing practical wisdom.[9]

In her general description, Hursthouse claims that a person who has practical wisdom "attains 'practical truth'; that is, he gets things right in action in what we would call 'the moral sphere'" (Hursthouse 2006, 285). We might ask what kind of "truth" practical wisdom gives us. Aristotle argues that experience is required for practical wisdom. No matter how smart or how much natural virtue a person has, it is impossible to have practical wisdom before a person acquires a certain amount of real world experience (Hursthouse 2006, 288). How does experience cultivate moral knowledge? Hursthouse explains that one way this happens is by learning about more complex moral experiences. The more inexperienced may have a kind of natural virtue, but, to properly express full virtue, the inexperienced need practice learning when and how to allow exceptions. In other words, the less experienced are prone to apply virtues too generally or methodically, but, by learning from example or coming to understand the good reasons for seemingly anomalous situations, the young develop a more complex understanding of the virtues. Gibbs argues for a similar kind of moral development from experience for both empathy and our understanding of reciprocity (which is related to justice).

In our practice of empathy, it is difficult for the young to understand situations of mixed emotion. Until we reach a certain level of cognitive development, we can only consider one thing at a time so we will focus on the most immediate. Later, we are able to consider multiple factors or viewpoints at once—which leads to a more complex understanding of both empathy and justice. For example, a young person visiting a terminally ill friend in the hospital may laugh uproariously at the person's wry joke—completely missing the melancholy undertones. Later, the person would respond appropriately (which may or may not include laughing at said joke), but his demeanor would also continue to reflect the seriousness of the occasion.

Gibbs argues that experiential learning is especially important for our conceptions of reciprocity as it relates to justice. Due to immature cognitive development and natural egocentrism, young children have a very rigid, pragmatic view of reciprocity. Whatever you do to me, I do to you. For example, if we are drawing and you accidentally draw a line through my picture, the appropriate response is for you to allow me to draw a line through your picture. This eye-for-an-eye version of reciprocity fails to account for the complexity of social relations. As Gibbs states, "Mature morality penetrates through superficial considerations of immature morality . . . to infer the intangible bases of interpersonal relationships or society" (Gibbs 2003, 54). Through experience, we come to understand the more complex nature of give and take not just in specific interpersonal relationships, but also in society. Gibbs terms this more mature version ideal moral reciprocity and it is cultivated through experiences of perspective taking. [10]

To better understand the kind of practical wisdom learned through appropriate experiences, let us briefly consider how this can go wrong. Hursthouse admits that some skills related to practical wisdom—such as cleverness or a keen ability to read other people—can also be used for wicked ends. Consider the example of a conman. This person is certainly skilled in reading people and situations. He understands how other people think and feel as well as how they are likely to react in certain situations. He also knows how others will "read" a specific situation and uses this to his advantage. For example, suppose our conman approaches a sympathetic stranger pretending to be a lost tourist. The conman is holding a map and uses this as a way to get next to the sympathetic stranger so that he can steal the stranger's wallet. In this way, the conman has many of the skills necessary for virtuous action, but uses them for wicked ends. Indeed, the conman is likely to try to activate specific virtuous responses from another in order to use their virtuous action against them. For this reason, we must have not only an understanding of virtue, but also a commitment to being virtuous. [11] Similarly, Gibbs argues that "*ego strength serves morality insofar as it links mature and veridical moral perception to action*" (Emphasis in original. Gibbs 2003, 132). In other words, we must use our talents (here ego strength) toward moral goals.

As Gibbs explains it, veridical moral perception allows a person to see things correctly despite "biasing influences." This is similar to field independence in visual processing. For example, if you show a person a complex design, a person with field independence can still pick out a certain geometric shape. This is a kind of reorienting that allows the person to focus on what is important despite distractions. Similarly, a person with veridical moral perception can reorient and stay focused on the salient features of a moral situation in spite of distractions or biases—this time related to social pressures or norms. Consider these descriptions of what Gibbs calls a "Type B" personality (or someone who has veridical moral perception).

The relation we found between field independence and Moral Type B suggests that Moral Type B individuals are more likely to engage in prosocial activity because they are more able to discern a core injustice in a situation despite distortive, obscuring, or distracting influences from the social context or "field" of a social group. (Gibbs 2003, 119)

Here we see a kind of "truth" that allows one to get things right in the moral sphere. I would argue this is one kind of truth that relates to practical wisdom—namely, a kind of veridical moral perception that allows a person to focus on the salient moral features.

To help pull all of this together, let us consider the case of racism. Hursthouse uses this as an example of poor training in children. She notes how children will learn racism over many years on both the affective (e.g., children will adopt similar emotional responses to people and situations as their parents) and the cognitive (e.g., children are also given "reasons" for why certain people deserve to be treated in a certain way) (Hursthouse 2001, 115). We see this in an example Gibbs discusses of a fourteen-year-old white youth at a recently integrated high school in the 1970s. He readily joined with his friends in taunting the new black youth who had joined the school and, at first, had no issues with this behavior. However, this youth seems to have the moral tools to reform his behavior. Over time, he noticed how the black youth, "knew how to smile when it was rough going [from the taunts], and . . . walked straight and was polite" (Coles, The moral life of children, quoted in Gibbs 2003, 112). Eventually, the white youth came to see the other youth's humanity, which activated his empathic responses. In fact, his new view was so secure that he intervened when his fellow peers were escalating to the point of possible physical violence. Ultimately, the white youth befriended the black peer and his new (more veridical) moral perception led him to become an advocate against segregation.

Here we see the relationship between the affective and the cognitive. Initially, the white youth was comfortable taunting the black youth. Due to his racist upbringing, he thought this was "right" and he felt no emotional qualms. However, as he noticed the black youth's behavior, his attitude changed on both a cognitive and an affective level. He became uncomfortable with his (and his peers) behavior toward the other youth and, eventually, he was able to articulate the reasons why—namely, the humanity of the black youth made the taunts unwarranted. As he became more comfortable with his new view and actually pursued a friendship with the black youth, his cognitive understanding continued to grow to the point of recognizing the structural injustice of segregation. His veridical moral perception allowed him not only to do the correct thing (stop his peers from physically assaulting the black youth), but also to gain a more mature moral understanding of the broader social situation. I believe both of these aspects (the individual behavior and the connection to the broader social situation) illustrate a kind of practical wisdom that would be relevant to Aristotle's understanding. Indeed, he internalized these new attitudes/beliefs into a new (more virtuous) state-of-character.

As mentioned earlier, veridical moral perception also shares similarities with Sherman's critical discernment. Sherman argues that critical discernment begins early in habituation, but it also continues to develop and will be relevant for practical wisdom. For example, Sherman believes that the reciprocal relationship between critical discernment and practical wisdom implies deliberation about ends (Sherman 1989, 91). Monica Mueller gives a similar argument in her work on practical wisdom. Using Hannah Arendt's analysis of Eichmann and "thoughtlessness," she argues that practical wisdom must include reflection about ends or our proper understanding of the Good. Specifically, Mueller argues that we should use Arendt's distinction between spectator and actor or the idea that we can reflect on our past actions by considering how they would be viewed by others (i.e., a "spectator"). We should also try to consider as many views as possible. Arendt calls this "thinking without banisters" or rejecting the idea that there is one universal opinion. Drawing on these aspects of Arendt's theory, Mueller argues that practical wisdom requires critical reflection. We must reflect not only on how to do the right thing, but what is the right thing to do.

> I suggest that the grasping—when one "sees" what they think is right to do in this situation here and now—involves a judgment accepted previously in reflection, which becomes relevant in the perceptive apprehension of a current experience. This reflective endorsement and the perceptive apprehension of the particulars together constitute thinking without banisters in a moment demanding action, and this is imperative for good action in circumstances where cultural and social guideposts have collapsed. (Mueller 2013, 18)

Consider this description of practical wisdom in relation to the white teen we discussed earlier. He used empathy and critical reflection to attain a more veridical moral perception. Ultimately he comes to "see" the connection between his previously held beliefs about how to treat *people* and the black student's *humanity*. Therefore, in moral development, we should encourage reflective judgment that includes taking the spectator role—including as many perspectives as possible.

THE ROLE OF "PROPER" UPBRINGING IN DEVELOPING A VIRTUOUS CHARACTER

We can now see how moral development theory helps explain the relationship between habituation, state-of-character, and practical wisdom. Without appropriate inductions in discipline encounters, a child will not be able (or at least will have a much more difficult time) dampening his natural egocentrism so he can cultivate proper empathic responses. We see now how this relates to both the affective and the cognitive. On the affective level, a child needs to learn to pay attention to natural empathic tendencies and to learn things like self-control. On the cognitive level, a child must learn to attend to the salient features of a situation or veridical moral perception and to respond with an appropriate action. In virtue theory, this later component would relate to proper expression of the virtues. Eventually, the affective and cognitive must come together in the proper way if one is to develop a virtuous state-of-character and the practical wisdom that goes with it.

We also see that the empirical evidence seems to support the cognitivist theory. For example, neuroscience research also posits an interconnection between feeling and thought or the cognitive components of affect (Damasio 2005, 2000). In relation to my project here, I think this debate also has something interesting to say about parenting styles. While I hope to accommodate a variety of approaches to parenting—I do not believe there is one specific way to be a virtuous parent—there are times that the arguments and/or empirical research lead us in a certain direction. In this case, both the theoretical and empirical work seems to support an authoritative parenting style over both authoritarian and overly permissive parenting styles.

For induction to be successful, the parent needs to find the right balance in the use of parental power. Parents are clearly powerful figures in the child's life. In attempting to redirect the child in a way that activates appropriate empathic responses, parents need to use enough power to get the child's attention but not so much power that the child becomes more concerned with the use of power than the lesson the parent is attempting to teach. Deciding on the appropriate use of power will be context dependent. Was the child's behavior intentional or merely negligent? Does the child readily respond to parental intervention or does it take more effort to get the child to notice? However, within this framework, a median approach between authoritarian and overly permissive styles seems to be the most appropriate way to hit the mark.

> Discipline that emphasizes power does not cultivate empathy; indeed, unqualified power assertion fosters in the child self-focused concerns with external consequences, which can in turn *reduce* prosocial behavior. Severe levels of power assertion, or physical child abuse, can inculcate in the child a schema or internal working model of the world as dangerous and threatening, of others as having hostile intentions; such biased or distorted social information processing has been linked to subsequent antisocial behavior. In contrast, inductive discipline elicits empathic distress and empathy-based transgression guilt by directing the child to consider how his or her behavior has affected others. The elicited empathic affect charges or renders "hot" the other-oriented induction,

> empowering it to prevail over egoistic motives in subsequent moral situations.
> (Emphasis in original. Gibbs 2003, 103)

Here we can see how authoritative parenting hits the mark. If the parent is overly permissive, he will likely not intervene at all or, if he does, the attempt will be too meager to demand the child's attention. The child soon realizes he is in control and not the parent. However, if the parent is too authoritarian and, thus, emphasizes the use of power to make the child comply, then the child becomes focused on the parent and not the situation. Gibbs, using Hoffman, also emphasizes that refocusing the child's attention *requires explanations*. This helps the child "decenter" (i.e., let go of her ego-centrism) and better understand the perspective of the other. Authoritarian parents are less likely to give explanations or engage the child in discussion. Authoritarian parenting tends more toward the "because I said so" approach.

If we return to the theories of habituation we discussed earlier, we can see how the mechanical view tends toward an authoritarian parenting style while the cognitivist view implies a more authoritative style. Recall that Steutel and Spiecker view habituation as a form of conditioning. The child learns right and wrong and the appropriate affective responses through a process of reinforcement (pleasure) and punishment (pain). Not only does the child want to avoid the pain of punishment and increase the pleasure of affirmation, but, since the child presumably has a loving relationship with the tutor/parent, he will eventually adopt or internalize the same cares and concerns as the parent. I believe this reflects a more authoritarian style of parenting because it emphasizes the controlling aspects of discipline (using punishment and reinforcement to get children to comply) while ignoring the role of explanation or directed reflection that is key to engaging the child's empathic responses. [12] As our other mechanical theorist, Curzer, explains "learners come to desire virtuous acts for their own sake not through the pleasure of virtuous action . . . but rather through the pain of punishment" (Curzer 2002, 159). This view seems to leave no room for the guidance associated with authoritative parenting.

In contrast, the engagement with the cognitive aspects of emotion in Sherman's theory seem to require a more authoritative parenting style. Recall that the parent helps the child develop critical discernment through directed reflection and explanation.

> First, as we shall see, though the child's reasons will be borrowed in varying degrees from outside, they will also be generated internally by the child's own perceptions, beliefs, and feelings. These, *in dialogue with the beliefs of an experienced adult*, will shape desire. (Emphasis added. Sherman 1989, 164)

Although getting the child to comply surely has a place, we can see that Sherman emphasizes dialogue or the learning process, not punishment. Also, in contrast to Curzer, Sherman emphasizes pleasure instead of pain. She argues that critical activity and enjoyment of that activity relate to all stages of development. Aristotle, according to Sherman, also believes that learning is always enjoyable to whatever degree a person is capable of partaking in it. Learning to be virtuous or more skill in virtuous activity is no different. This is how she explains the connection between pleasure and virtue.

> On the interpretation I shall offer, pleasure not only issues in but arises from discriminatory activity. The model I ascribe to Aristotle is thus that of a chain of activities which increase in discriminated complexity as well as in deriva-tive pleasures. On this model practice yields pleasure to the extent to which practice itself is critical. And pleasure, in turn, yields further critical activity. (Sherman 1989, 184)

In this way, learning virtue through habituation is a process of discernment that includes dialogue and reflection, not mere conditioning of responses. The pleasure gained from increased skill in the process not only helps to train our affective responses, but also to encourage children to continue.

To summarize, let me return to the example of young children and empathy. Gibbs argues that we have natural empathic tendencies, but—especially in our youth—our egocentrism will sometimes override the empathic re-sponses. An authoritative parent will take advantage of these teachable mo-ments. Rather than forcing the child to comply with threats of punishment, the authoritative parent will engage the child in an attempt to redirect the child's focus. The parent will point out how the child's actions lead to the other child's harm or distress; thereby, attempting to reengage the empathic responses. In this way, the parent is beginning to teach critical discernment or to train the child to focus on the morally salient aspects of the situation. If successful, eventually the child will begin to do this more and more on her own. As Sherman points out, this process is also supported by the pleasure of learning and, I would argue, the social pleasures. If we have natural tenden-cies to have empathic responses for other humans, then we also have natural tendencies to find helping others pleasurable. [13] Indeed, much of the current research on happiness supports this idea (*Happy. [Electronic Resource (Video)]* 2012). In this way, we can find the virtues pleasurable for their own sake and not just for what being virtuous can get us in life. However, as Sherman points out, Aristotle also thinks the pleasure of virtue needs to be related to virtue in the correct way—namely, developing a virtuous state-of-character and practical wisdom.

Again, empirical research explains how parents can help facilitate this kind of moral development. For example, Lawrence Walker and Karl Hennig conducted two longitudinal studies where they recorded discussions of moral dilemmas between parents and children and then tracked the children's moral growth. Discussions included both hypothetical and real-life situations. Their conclusions also favor authoritative parenting over authoritarian parenting.

> Again, the stimulation of higher-level moral reasoning, along with a gentle Socratic style of representational interactions, seems to readily promote moral development; whereas the more conflictual operational and interfering style of interactions provides an environment that retards growth. (Walker and Hennig 1999, 370)

Parents who were hostile, critical, and rigid impeded moral development; while parents who engaged the children in dialogue promoted moral growth. It is easy to see why this would be the case when we consider the nature of these parent/child interactions. The authoritative parents encouraged children to share their opinions and their process of moral reasoning. This not only has affective components (i.e., showing the children that their view is important or matters), but also cognitive components (i.e., beginning a reflection on moral reasoning). It also allowed the parents to share their (presumably more expert) moral reasoning. In these ways, parents modeled a kind of critical reflection necessary for developing veridical moral perception and practical wisdom.

BRINGING IT ALL TOGETHER

Focusing on the *Nicomachean Ethics*, M. F. Burnyeat gives an overview of Aristotle's understanding of moral development. He is interested in the importance of good upbringing or explaining how we get from habituation to practical wisdom. Ultimately, he outlines various stages of moral development related to types of value. Aristotle discusses three types of value—pleasure, the noble, and the advantageous or good. Burnyeat posits that stages of moral development are related to learning to appreciate these various types of value.

> There are three irreducibly distinct categories of value for the fully virtuous man to get right—the three we have been discussing. Pursuit of pleasure is an inborn part of our animal nature; concern for the noble depends on good upbringing; while the good, here specified as the advantageous, is the object of mature relation. We have seen that each of the three categories connects with a distinct set of desires and feelings, which acquire motivating affect at different stages of development. (Burnyeat 1981, 86)

The young are prone to follow pleasure, through good upbringing they begin to pursue the noble, and, eventually, with proper development of the intellect in coordination with desire, they will strive for the good. Yet, we should avoid a rigid distinction between these categories. As Burnyeat points out, the fully virtuous man will take pleasure in what is noble so, in this way, categories can overlap.

Considering our current discussion, we could roughly map habituation, state-of-character, and practical wisdom onto these categories. In youth we find value in pleasure so we use habituation to train the young to find pleasure in the right things. As Sherman argues, learning is pleasurable. Therefore, the child will take pleasure in increasing her skills of discernment. Here we can see how one begins to transition from habituation to state-of-character. As Gibbs and Hursthouse point out, children will eventually internalize norms. As this occurs, the youth has a vested interest in living up to those norms or acting virtuously. As this state-of-character becomes more ingrained or stable, the person will want to act virtuously not simply for the pleasure it brings, but also out of a sense of identity. It is part of who she is. She will also develop a more complex understanding of justice and, thus, want to do the right thing because it is right. Here we see how a young adult begins to value the noble or acting for the sake of virtue. Finally, we gain the experience that leads to practical wisdom. As our discussion shows, practical wisdom relates not only to better deliberation about right actions but also includes some reflection on our ends or the Good. Thus, practical wisdom leads us to value the Good—otherwise why would we work toward it?

NOTES

1. For an example of how these judgments work on both the individual and the cultural level, see Marilyn Frye's "On Anger" (Frye 1983).

2. This is similar to Rosalind Hursthouse's discussion of "good comprehension" in relation to practical wisdom—which I address in more detail in the next chapter (Hursthouse 2006).

3. It should be noted that I am intentionally exaggerating the distinction between "biological" and "cognitive" components here to emphasize the cognitive aspects that are especially important to our discussion.

4. Indeed, many theories argue that we need to be careful of the fine line between guilt and shame. Shame leads to defensiveness that shuts down reflection whereas guilt allows for reflection and retribution. For this reason, many parenting books emphasize that parents should focus on the behaviors, not the person (e.g., "Your actions harmed David" versus "You are a bad boy").

5. Kerr argues that the mechanical view suffers from what she calls an intellectualist bias or "a tendency to equate cognition primarily or even exclusively with the intellect, and to overlook deny, or disparage other forms of cognitive activity" (Kerr 2011, 647).

6. Benson actually has a couple versions of this theory—a strong version (which I use here) and a weaker version that he develops in a later article (Benson 1994). In the later article, he also distances himself from this original theory, but I think the stronger version is more applicable to our analysis of virtue theory.

7. I do not have the space for an extended discussion of how appreciation for the "noble" ties into a virtuous character. However, one analysis that shares some parallels with the view I am tentatively proposing here would be Stephen Darwall's *Rational Care and Welfare* (Darwall 2002).

8. It goes beyond the scope of this book to consider the ontological status of affective responses (biological versus cognitive, etc.). All we need to notice here is that mature moral

empathy (and other mature moral responses) includes both affective ("passions" or emotions) and cognitive (reasoning or rational) components.

9. This is a preliminary discussion of practical wisdom. Here I focus on practical wisdom in relation to moral development. In the next chapter, I revisit the concept of practical wisdom to consider what it means in relation to parenting.

10. In her rethinking of practical wisdom, Monica Mueller also emphasizes the development of the ability to consider multiple perspectives (Mueller 2013).

11. One could ask what it means to have "a commitment to being virtuous." All this means is that a person is trying to cultivate the virtues or be a virtuous person. As the example here shows, there are many practical skills associated with developing a virtuous character that could also be used for more nefarious ends. Virtue theorists recognize this and, in response, add the caveat that we should have a commitment to being virtuous. As the next sentence shows, moral psychologists make a similar caveat.

12. In their discussion of Sherman, they do seem to allow some role for cultivating discernment, but they seem to want to deny that it is connected to the process of habituation.

13. Research with young children shows that we might also have a natural tendency toward spite. For example, in experiments, children would forgo an opportunity to get candy if it meant also giving another child more candy than the deciding child would get. However, since most of these experiments relate to unfairness (or a kind of injustice), I think they say more about our developing sense of justice than a natural tendency to help or hurt fellow humans (Bloom 2013).

Chapter Two

Parental Wisdom

It is often said that parents know their children better than anyone else. Ideally, I think this is true. The constant give and take of many parent-child relationships lends itself to a kind of knowledge about another that we rarely get in other relationships.[1] In fact, I argue that the knowledge parents can gain about their children often leads to a kind of practical wisdom. Obviously, Aristotle's conception of practical wisdom is broader than the application I use here. However, if practical wisdom is necessary for acting virtuously and parenting can be a kind of virtuous activity, then I think we can consider how practical wisdom applies to the activity of parenting. I will explain this in a way that I think is mostly compatible with Aristotle's conception, but I also move beyond his original concept to incorporate modern philosophical theories of the virtues and skills of parenting.

Let me begin with a few clarifications. First, Aristotle often describes practical wisdom in a way that makes it seem an impossible ideal for everyday people. In response, some scholars make a distinction between "perfect wisdom" and "real world wisdom" (Swartwood 2013). I too want practical wisdom to be an attainable goal. As most of Aristotle's theory works on a kind of continuum, it does not seem unreasonable to say that parents (or anyone) can exercise a certain degree of practical wisdom even if they are not perfectly wise and never make mistakes. I believe this is especially true if we consider the various skills or components of practical wisdom.

Second, Aristotle's conception of practical wisdom is complex and I have no hope for settling the variety of debates around this conception here. What I propose to do is use some theories about practical wisdom to help explain the kinds of knowledge and wisdom that parents often use. Let's begin with the basics. Practical wisdom is a kind of knowledge that is intermingled with the empirical. Aristotle also characterizes it as a kind of deliberation that includes both affective and cognitive components. Finally, developing practical wisdom takes time and a variety of life experiences. Practical wisdom is not a technical skill that can be strictly taught like carpentry, but it definitely involves skills. To begin to understand the interplay between knowledge of the virtues, skills necessary for practical wisdom, and the kind of experience needed, I begin with Rosalind Hursthouse's analysis of practical wisdom. I will assume that most parents are interested in doing right by their children so I appreciate that Hursthouse focuses on the difference between a person with practical wisdom and a person with natural virtue (instead of the wicked or incontinent). In her description, Hursthouse argues that, in addition to the prerequisite knowledge of the virtues, practical wisdom requires correct discernment, good comprehension, and good deliberation.

Hursthouse notes that Aristotle's account of correct discernment is very brief, "correct judgment of what is reasonable/equitable/decent" (Hursthouse 2006, 290–91). Her explanation emphasizes learning when exceptions are appropriate instead of rigidly applying our paradigmatic conception of virtue.

> It is only with the experience of exceptions—when an admired figure does what you thought only a pusillanimous coward would do and is widely praised, when the action of someone you respect surprises you until she explains why she did it, when you hear accounts of such examples—that you come to the more sophisticated understanding—the discernment—that the *phronimos* has. And, as you develop the discernment, you develop the practical *nous*. (Hursthouse 2006, 292)

Correct discernment is closely related to good comprehension—both are a kind of judgment. However, a lack of correct discernment is more like a kind of naiveté whereas good comprehension relates to getting the facts of the matter correct.

As Hursthouse explains, good comprehension has to do with understanding what kind of situation is presented to me. It is very easy to go wrong here because we often have to rely on the accounts of others.

> We should, I think, allow ourselves to be struck by how *often* finding out exactly what "the situation" is, with a view to acting well, involves judging what other people say, particularly about their own, or someone else's, actions and/or feelings, past, present or future. (Emphasis in original. Hursthouse 2006, 293)

Here experience relates to figuring out who to trust and how to decipher the variety of information with which we are presented. Clearly, this requires experience with relationships and specific people.

Finally, we need good deliberation or deciding on the "most fine" or "effective" means to our end. Here the less experienced may be more clumsy in their attempts to be virtuous. For example, Hursthouse presents the case of a child who floats out into the river current. One with natural virtue may immediately jump in the water and try to swim toward the child. This person may or may not accomplish her goal depending on the strength of the current and her skills as a swimmer. One who is practically wise might run up the river bank to get ahead of the child before jumping into the river. This will give her an advantage in catching up with the child and improve her chances for a successful rescue. In this way, the person with practical wisdom knows the most effective way to accomplish the virtuous goal. This kind of example also reiterates that we are not discussing "good" versus "bad" parents. Hursthouse's starting point is natural virtue, and I start with the assumption that parents have good intentions or (to use Aristotle's language) a desire to be virtuous. Here we are simply contemplating what kinds of wisdom or skills might help parents to "get things right" more often than not.

Before moving on, one last point about good deliberation. While this case involved practical knowledge, in other cases it may be difficult to decide how to proceed at all. For example, Hursthouse proposes a situation where a child is addicted to drugs. Clearly, one would want to intervene in a helpful way, but how best to begin this process? Should the parent confront the child or take a more indirect approach? Is tough love the best option or a more nurturing attitude? Thus, good deliberation requires knowledge about the way the world works, but also experience with relationships and people.

With this initial description in mind, consider a simple case to see how practical wisdom applies to the everyday experience of parenthood. Ben is a young child who is supposed to be getting ready for bed. The routine is the same every night, so Ben clearly knows what he is supposed to do—take off his clothes and put them in the hamper, put on his pajamas, and brush his teeth. Sarah, his mom, is also busy organizing things for the next morning and getting ready for bedtime. When Sarah checks in, Ben is sitting on the edge of the bed staring into space—in other words, he appears to be doing nothing. The first thing Sarah must do is accurately comprehend "the situation." Is Ben being willfully disobedient or is he simply exhausted and, thus, easily distracted? How she assesses the situation will influence her discernment and deliberation. Suppose she knows Ben is particularly upset about bedtime tonight and, thus, decides he is being willfully disobedient. Her response is to sternly remind him of his responsibilities. The situation continues to escalate and eventually Ben is sanctioned with a penalty—no video games tomorrow. If she has accurately assessed the situation, Ben will likely continue to be upset, but may grudgingly accept his fate as he knew what he was doing. If she has inaccurately assessed the situation, he may suddenly break down in tears and have a total meltdown. In which case, Sarah belatedly realizes that Ben was actually exhausted and, in fact, beginning to get sick. Instead of escalating the situation, Sarah should have correctly discerned that this was a situation that required an exception. Instead of reinforcing Ben's need to take responsibility for himself, she should have stepped in and helped him through the process to get him to bed and the rest he so desperately needs. Alternately, Sarah may also have good comprehension (Ben is exhausted) and correctly discerned the situation (so she should make an exception to the normal level of self-management she requires from her six-year-old) and still made a mistake in deliberation. Perhaps she steps in and begins to help Ben put on his pajamas. At this point, Ben has a meltdown because he wanted to do it himself (even though he was currently distracted) so the most effective route would have been a form of gentle prodding (by making a game of the routine) instead of simply taking over the situation.

In this example, we see how a seemingly simple situation can be full of complex decisions that require the variety of skills associated with practical wisdom. Sarah must have a good comprehension of the situation (disobedience or exhaustion?) which will hopefully lead her to a correct discernment about what kind of response is needed (frustration or compassion?). She must also have good deliberation about the most efficient means to accomplish her goal/end (reprimand or assistance?). To further elaborate on these connections, I turn now to the general goals of maternal work outlined by Sarah Ruddick in *Maternal Thinking*—preservative love, fostering growth, and training for social acceptance.[2] Preservative love relates to maternal protectiveness or keeping children safe. However, it must be balanced with fostering growth or allowing children to mature and develop into independent adults. Finally, parents must work within specific cultural demands. If children are to be part of the community, they must also have a certain level of social acceptance. I believe all three of these goals require practical wisdom as explained in the skills outlined by Hursthouse. In what follows, I use Ruddick as a starting point to outline the main idea behind each parental commitment, but then go on to complicate Ruddick's initial understanding. In my analysis, I hope to provide a more nuanced understanding of how parents try to achieve these goals—sometimes in very trying circumstances. The discussion will also highlight the kinds of wisdom parents must draw on in sorting out how to best meet these commitments.

PRESERVATIVE LOVE

Since all three of the maternal commitments Ruddick outlines relate to each other, the distinctions in these three sections are somewhat artificial. Here I focus on preservative love, but briefly introduce fostering growth to show how they are connected. Ruddick argues that preservation is the preeminent demand that children make on parents. She seems to mostly have in mind the period of prolonged dependence for human children. "Preserving the lives of children is the central constitutive, invariant aim of maternal practice; the commitment to achieving that aim is the constitutive maternal act" (Ruddick 1989, 19). While she acknowledges that preservation continues as children get older, preservation takes precedence over the other commitments when children are infants. As children grow and begin to develop personalities, parents turn more attention to fostering growth—specifically, nurturing children's emotional and intellectual growth.

As she fleshes out her understanding, Ruddick tries to acknowledge that some mothers may face greater difficulties in their attempts at preservation, but this does not seem to be her main focus.

> With adequate care, and barring disasters, children do not die. . . . To be sure, many mothers suffer from poverty and violence; caring requires of them superordinate efforts against great odds. But in a politically decent and minimally prosperous society, children become cooperative partners in their own well-being. (Ruddick 1989, 71)

While she continues to occasionally hand wave to these more trying circumstances, much of her discussion seems to assume this "politically decent and minimally prosperous" society. Yet, as we know, many do *not* live in the kind of society Ruddick envisions.

Violence is a significant component of oppression and many marginalized groups must deal with the threat of violence to their families and children. This reality is acknowledged by Patricia Hill Collins when she declares that protection is a preoccupation for black mothers (Collins 2000, 197). In thinking about the relationship between preservation and growth, black mothers must socialize their children for survival in a culture that is hostile to their very existence. In response to these demands, Collins argues that black mothers must prepare their daughters to be self-sufficient and for the kinds of work they are likely to do, but at the same time try to prepare them to go further than the mothers, themselves, have.

> Black daughters must learn how to survive the sexual politics of intersecting oppressions while rejecting and transcending these same power relations. In order to develop these skills in their daughters, mothers demonstrate varying combinations of behaviors devoted to ensuring their daughters' survival—such as providing them with basic necessities and protecting them in dangerous environments—to helping their daughters go further than mothers themselves were allowed to go (Joseph 1981, 1984). They remain simultaneously visionary about what is possible, yet pragmatic about what it might take to get there (James and Busia 1993). (Collins 2000, 184)

Recent mainstream attention to police brutality against the African American community shows that this continues to be a pressing issue for black families. "It's the fact that for the entire Black community in our society, there is a calculus to be made about one's children that's not prevalent among whites. It's the knowledge that your child might be stolen away by the very people who should be protecting him or her" (Cross 2014). While it does not get as much attention in the mainstream media, this is also a significant issue for other marginalized groups such as Native American peoples and the Latino/a community (Cross 2014; Dill 1988).

This systemic violence makes finding the balance between preservative love and fostering growth that much more complicated. As Sarah Brown so eloquently puts it:

> I think about how often I keep you near me and how many people take umbrage with that. *She has to learn,* they say, *how to live in this world.* But how can you learn at 4 to do what still makes me flail and falter at 34? And how can I let you go when a girl a year younger than you was gunned down in our city last week and a boy who would've headed off to college for the first time on Monday was executed within steps of his Ferguson, MO home on Saturday? (Emphasis in original. Brown 2014)

These examples help show the complicated and sometimes fraught relationship between preservation and growth. It also calls for specific kinds of wisdom.

While Aristotle's conception of practical wisdom recognizes the interplay between affective or emotional components and reason, these examples lead us to a kind of lived knowledge that Aristotle does not discuss—embodied knowledge. Again, Collins explains:

> These theorists suggest that women are more likely to experience two modes of knowing: one located in the body and the space it occupies and the other passing beyond it. Through multiple forms of mothering, women mediate these two modes and use the lived experiences of their daily lives to assess more abstract knowledge claims (D. Smith 1987). (Collins 2000, 259)

In this way, the experience of living in an oppressive society is encoded in a specific way. Although Ruddick admits that warnings about danger often carry an emotional resonance that helps children internalize the message (Ruddick 1989, 69), I do not think her analysis fully captures the kind of wisdom black mothers are trying to pass on to their children in the form of survival skills. This is an attitude of deep suspicion that is a kind of wariness against a racist society. A kind of embodied wisdom that Katie Cannon describes in this way:

> You know where the minefields are . . . there is wisdom. . . . You are in touch with the ancestors . . . and it is from the gut, not rationally figured out. Black women have to use this all the time, of course, the creativity is still there, but we are not fools . . . we call it "the epistemological privileges of the op-

pressed." How do you tap that wisdom—name it, mine it, pass it on to the next generation? (Cannon 1995, 11)

In sum, raising children in a violently racist society requires multiple kinds of wisdom. Parents must understand the nature of intersecting oppressions and the threats they represent to their children. However, parents must also pass on specific kinds of wisdom to their children such as how to navigate these situations (as best as possible). In thinking about both these kinds of wisdom we are moving beyond the kind of knowledge and wisdom that Aristotle recognized. In this last quote we see a kind of wisdom that is both embodied and can be (must be) taught.

FOSTERING GROWTH

As our previous discussion shows there is a close (perhaps even reciprocal) relationship between preservation and fostering growth. However, if we think about the variety of things to which fostering growth may apply, we also see specific connections between this commitment and practical wisdom. First, a fuller description of what fostering growth entails. As Ruddick explains:

> To foster growth, then, is to sponsor or nurture a child's unfolding, expanding material spirit. Children demand this nurturance because their development is complex, gradual, and subject to distinctive kinds of distortion or inhibition. . . . *The mind of a mother fostering growth is marked by a sense of children's complexity and of the difficulties of responding confidently to them.* (Emphasis added. Ruddick 1989, 83)

We see from this description that fostering growth requires a great deal of knowledge. One must have some idea of the basic aspects of childhood development, experience with the personality of your specific child, and an awareness of the changing nature of the child as she ages.

As Ruddick points out a key difficulty here is knowing when to intervene and, if so, in what way. For example, suppose a parent has a child who begins to have terrible nightmares. Is this simply a phase? There are times in the development of young children when the imagination will become very vivid. Young children also sometimes have trouble distinguishing reality from fantasy. Perhaps the nightmares are simply a normal stage of development and all the child needs is a sense of security and loving reassurance. On the other hand, the nightmares could also be the result of something else. Perhaps the young child is developing unhealthy levels of anxiety. Or something happened (or is continuing to happen) at daycare that this parent should know about and address. In this case, the parent may need to intervene in a more direct and methodical way. This is an example of the delicate balance in fostering growth.

Notice also that, in this example, a key component is understanding your child. As Hursthouse points out, good comprehension often relates to understanding the motives, intentions, and reasoning of other people. Similarly, Ruddick argues that mothers must consider the connection and relationship between body and mind. Specifically, mothers cannot read their children via behaviors alone, they must also consider what is going on mentally for the child. For both Hursthouse and Ruddick this is often a process of trial and error. Mothers will test out responses to see if their interpretations are correct or how to most effectively achieve their goals. Again, we see why experience is necessary for practical wisdom. As Hursthouse states, "The experience might be of one's own failures or of learning about others'. Or it might be of learning about others' successful methods" (Hursthouse 2006, 305). There is a reason parents love to share stories (and why parenting books are such a popular genre).

This also points to one of the key skills of parenthood—attentive love. Attentive love "knits together maternal thinking, designates a cognitive capacity—attention—and a virtue—love" (Ruddick 1989, 119). Again, we see the parallels with our general account of practical wisdom. One appealing aspect of Aristotle's virtue ethics is the way he blends cognitive and affective components. Virtue requires knowledge and reasoning, but we must also have the correct feelings. What separates the virtuous from the continent is that the virtuous person does not just perform the correct action, but also takes pleasure in the right things. Without getting into a meta-ethical debate over how well various moral theories incorporate this insight, I think this aspect of virtue theory (and practical wisdom) is very relevant to thinking about parenthood. It is an insightful way of thinking about how parents should approach children and the goals of parenthood. Often my analysis of practical wisdom tends to sound like parents are detached problem solvers trying to decide what to do with the clay before them. I want to avoid this impression and some analysis of attentive love is one way to work the emotive component back into our discussion.

Drawing on the work of Iris Murdoch and Simone Weil, Ruddick argues that attentive love requires seeing the child for who she really is, not losing oneself in fantasy or projections of what we want the child to be. In this way, the parent must understand and know her child, but also be accepting of who the child is. At heart, we hope the parent/child relationship is based in love, trust, and other positive emotions. Yet, it is still the case that parenting can be hard work and the complex and multiple goals require a variety of knowledge and experiences. So my discussion of attentive love has two goals— one, to highlight the interplay between the affective and cognitive components of virtuous action; two, to illustrate a key source of experience that helps parents develop practical wisdom. Learning to "read" your child helps with good comprehension which makes it more likely one will also have correct discernment and good deliberation.

I believe that attentive love is more important than specific knowledge about childhood development. I want to be careful not to over-intellectualize parenthood. Practical wisdom is a kind of everyday knowledge, and attentive love is one way to gain the kind of knowledge needed for the practical wisdom of parenthood. Even parents who are not likely to study books on childhood development can learn to "read" their children in a very sophisticated way. As a result, they may be able to discern intentions, moods, and traits. They are also likely to know when something is wrong or "off" even if they do not immediately know what to do about it. To further elaborate these connections, let us consider another analysis of practical wisdom. Jason Swartwood argues that practical wisdom involves a skill set similar to the one used by experts that includes intuitive ability, deliberative ability, meta-cognitive ability, self-regulative ability, and self-cultivation ability. To help explain the importance of attentive love, I will consider each of the skills Swartwood proposes in relation to our discussion of parenthood.

Much as we would expect, intuitive ability means a person can identify what to do quickly without conscious reasons. Given the role of deliberation in practical wisdom, it may seem odd to propose intuition as a related skill. Yet, scholars admit that there are times when immediate action is called for and practical wisdom may come into play. As Hursthouse explains, the difference between the practically wise and the naturally virtuous in these situations has to do with having the right kind of knowledge or experience. For example, intuition can relate to the experience and knowledge parents have about their children that well-meaning strangers may not. Suppose John is at a soccer game and his son, Jason, makes a winning goal. John knows that Jason is a bit shy and does not like overly exuberant praise. When Jason comes to the side line John congratulates him with a high-five—Jason is pleased and happy. Soon, another parent from the team comes over yelling congratulations and going on and on about how excited she was and how proud she is of Jason. Now Jason immediately withdraws and merely gives her a weak smile. In this way, having the right kind of knowledge and experience allows the practically wise parent to intuitively get things right in a number of everyday situations.

Swartwood's discussion of deliberation parallels our earlier discussion of deliberation so I will skip that component and move on to his next skill—a meta-cognitive ability to discern when to use intuition and when to use deliberation. In common situations that the practically wise person has already reasoned through, intuition works well. However, when the expert or practically wise person is faced with an anomalous situation, she must use deliberation to sort out what to do. While this distinction may seem obvious, that is not always the case.

> Because intuitive and deliberative abilities will need to be coordinated in order to utilize them efficiently and effectively, a person needs meta-cognitive ability. Sometimes intuition will lead us astray without more deliberation, and sometimes deliberation is an unnecessary or corrupting influence on an intuitive identification of what to do. An expert needs to be able to tell the difference in the situations she's faced with. (Swartwood 2013, 521)

As we can see, Swartwood's argument here is very similar to Hursthouse's analysis of good comprehension. In order to get things right, we need to know what kind of situation presents itself to us or, given the nature of children's development, realize when the situation has changed and we need to deliberate about a new way to approach the situation. For example, suppose when Jane's daughter Emily comes home from school she is uncommunicative and immediately goes off to her room to listen to the radio. Should Jane rely on intuition or deliberation here? Intuition would say Emily is simply tired from a long day and needs some time to herself before dinner—in which case Jane should simply leave her alone. However, what if it is something else? Perhaps something troubling happened at school today and Emily needs to talk about it, but she cannot figure out how to start the conversation with her mother. In this case, Jane should seek Emily out and try harder to engage her. She would need to use deliberation to figure out how to get Emily to open up. Depending on what the situation actually is, Jane could make these worse if she does not correctly comprehend what is going on. If Emily really needs quiet time and Jane continues to try and engage her, Emily will become more annoyed and agitated. If Emily really needs to talk and Jane leaves her be, Jane may miss an opportunity to help Emily work through a difficult issue (and Emily may feel abandoned). Jane needs to correctly understand the situation to appropriately respond—is this a normal afternoon wind down session (in which case intuition is appropriate) or is it something more (in which case deliberation is necessary)?

The next aspect of Swartwood's skill set is particularly interesting for parenthood. He claims that a person with self-regulative ability will be able "to identify reliably how to affect the environment, her behavior, emotions and motivations so that she can successfully do what she has identified she ought to do" (Swartwood 2013, 519). For his example, he discusses a professional volleyball player who identifies, evaluates, and commits to practice and performance goals. Experts in sports or the arts must have self-regulative abilities that allow them to hone their craft and continually perform at a high level. I would argue that a main skill for parenting is cultivating a practice of attentive love. In our relationship with adults this is not a skill we often practice. We expect adults to take responsibility for themselves and, if we misjudge their actions, they are likely to tell us. While it is true that we may encounter a specific person who mystifies us so we spend more time and attention trying to decipher his motives or intentions, this is not the way we commonly approach peers in our day-to-day life. In this way, learning to "read" our children is a skill parents must cultivate. Some of the specific skills related to attentive love may include patience, reflective thinking, trial and error, and sustained focus. We are all caught up in our daily routines and many competing demands for our time and attention. As Ruddick points out, no parent could do this all the time:

> Mothers could not give, nor do children need, constant attentive love. What children and mothers require of each other is proper trust. Through the discipline of attentive love, a mother tries to make herself trustworthy. By training herself to "really look," she learns to trust a child she loves and to love a real, and therefore trustworthy, child. (Ruddick 1989, 123)

If a parent is to develop the practical wisdom that helps him "get things right," then the parent must cultivate the tendency to approach his child with attentive love. In other words, parents must spend at least some time learning how to "read" their children and learning when this skill will be necessary—this knowledge and experience are key components of the practical wisdom of parenthood. We could also tie this back to the meta-cognitive ability to shift between intuition and deliberation. As children grow and develop, they change. As they change, parents may need to shift from intuition to deliberation in order to understand a child as he or she moves to a new developmental stage. Clearly, having the skills of attentive love will help a parent know when to shift between these modes.

Using Swartwood, we see how attentive love—a skill necessary for practical wisdom as a parental virtue—utilizes a number of other skills necessary for a kind of real world version of practical wisdom. We have seen how attentive love draws on each of the skills Swartwood proposes: intuitive ability, deliberative ability, meta-cognitive ability, and self-regulative ability. Ultimately, these all come together in Swartwood's final skill—self-cultivation ability (i.e., working on improving intuitive, deliberative, and self-regulative abilities).

With this basic description of how practical wisdom relates to fostering growth, let me now complicate things a bit. What exactly does Ruddick mean by fostering growth or how intensive should this process be? For example, the new norm for most middle-class parents is a form of "intensive mothering" that sees raising children as a kind of project that requires much time, energy, and attention. In *Unequal Childhoods*, Annette Lareau calls this a process of "concerted cultivation" and, as she describes it, the key elements include "an emphasis on the development of the child through organized activities, development of vocabulary through reasoning and reading, and active parent involvement in schooling and other institutions outside of the home" (Lareau 2003, 24). She contrasts this to the predominant childrearing style for working-class and poor families which she calls "accomplishment of natural growth." In this approach, parents "viewed children's development as unfolding spontaneously, as long as they were provided with comfort, food, shelter, and other basic support" (Lareau 2003, 238). I will say more about this difference in parenting styles in the next chapter, I introduce it here merely to clarify the scope of fostering growth.

There are certainly times where Ruddick's understanding of fostering growth sounds closer to the more intensive cultivation favored by middle-class parents, but I do not believe we have to interpret this goal of parenting in that way. Ruddick points out that fostering growth also relates to more routine aspects of parenting. For example, part of fostering growth is simply creating a safe space in which that growth can happen. As Ruddick explains, "Home is where children are supposed to return when their world turns heartless, where they center themselves in the world they are discovering" (Ruddick 1989, 87). We see this echoed in the reflections of a poor mother who eventually threw her drug-addicted sister out of her house in order to maintain a safe space for her children.

> I [field worker] ask her, "Is she going to be moving?" She says firmly, "She is going to go." I say, "It is hard on your nerves." She says, "This is a house but it got to be a home." I say, "Where will she go?" She shakes her head (to indicate she doesn't know). She says, "The kids won't come in here when she is here." She asks me, "Did you ever notice that?" I nod slowly. She says, "I got to make this a home not a house." (Lareau 2003, 157)

The final straw for this mother was when she caught her sister stealing from her children. As we see in this quote, the mother is clearly focused on creating a safe and nurturing environment that can foster her children's growth.

Another ordinary aspect of fostering growth is simply helping children navigate the various emotional trials of growing up. Again, we see this in a variety of families despite differences in how they approach the task. In Lareau's work we see a middle-class mother helping her daughter cope with a particularly brusque gymnastics teacher. She does this both through discussions with her daughter and, sometimes, directly intervening (Lareau 2003, 172–77). In a different example, a working-class family has a daughter who is constantly pestered by a boy who sits behind her. The teacher seems unaware or uninterested in the fact that this boy constantly pulls her ponytail. The mother and father sympathize with her situation and advise her to punch him when the teacher isn't looking (Lareau 2003, 217). While these two families have different approaches to the problems, they are both clearly invested in helping their children learn how to deal with difficult situations.

It is worth noting that all of these examples also draw on the wisdom that comes from attentive love. Ms. McAllister noticed how her kids acted when her sister was around. Stacy's mom noticed how upset she was when she returned from gymnastics practice. In this way, we see how parents from a variety of backgrounds draw on the knowledge learned from this skill to help foster growth. However, attentive love is more than just noticing if your child is upset and helping her work through it. It also requires seeing your child for who he really is, not who you want him to be. We see this subtle distinction in a story from Audre Lorde about learning to help her son deal with bullying at school. At first, her own past clearly shapes her response.

> And when I heard that the ringleader was a little boy in Jonathan's class his own size, an interesting and very disturbing thing happened to me. My fury at my own long-ago impotence, and my present pain at his suffering, made me start to forget all that I knew about violence and fear, and blaming the victim, I started to hiss at the weeping child. "The next time you come in here crying . . .," and suddenly caught myself in horror. (Lorde 1984, 75)

In this moment, Lorde realizes that she is responding to her own past traumas as well as her inability to deal with her son's pain and fear. Yet, she is able to redirect her thoughts and find a more productive way to engage her son. She does this not only through attentive love (seeing him for who he really is and focusing on what he really needs), but also by drawing on the experience and wisdom of friends.

> And no, Jonathan didn't have to fight if he didn't want to, but somehow he did have to feel better about not fighting. An old horror rolled over me of being the fat kid who ran away, terrified of getting her glasses broken.
>
> About that time a very wise woman said to me, "Have you ever told Jonathan that once you used to be afraid, too?"
>
> The idea seemed far-out to me at the time, but the next time he came in crying and sweaty from having run away again, I could see that he felt shamed at having failed me, or some image he and I had created in his head of mother/woman.
>
> . . .
>
> I sat down on the hallway steps and took Jonathan in my lap and wiped his tears. "Did I ever tell you about how I used to be afraid when I was your age?"
>
> I will never forget the look on that little boy's face as I told him the tale of my glasses and my after-school fight. It was a look of relief and total disbelief, all rolled into one. (Lorde 1984, 76)

This example clearly illustrates the subtleties and nuances of attentive love. It also shows that while it is one key skill of practical wisdom for parenting, it is not the only skill. Parents can also draw on knowledge from other relatives, parents, and friends.

Again, I want to reiterate that I am starting with the assumption of natural goodness—most parents care about their children and want the best for them. The cases I have highlighted show this to be true across classes, races, and so forth. However, it is also the case that sometimes more education and resources can help parents in this endeavor. In this way, we can think about practical wisdom as it relates to fostering growth in two ways. First, attentive love helps parents understand the unique personality and needs of each individual child. All parents are capable of this kind of wisdom. Those who are economically stressed and must spend long hours working to earn enough money to meet basic needs may have less time for this than more privileged parents, but this does not mean that less privileged parents are unaware of this kind of knowledge or that the ability to cultivate it is directly tied to economic resources. For example, take this quote from a domestic worker who spent more time raising a white family's children than the biological parents did:

> I was more like a mother to them, and you see she didn't have to take too much time as a mother should to know her children. They were more used to me because I put them to bed. The only time she would actually be with them was like when I'm off Thursday and on Sundays. They would go out sometime, but actually I was really the mother because I raised them from little [Pearl Runner]. (Hale 1980, 121)

In this way, attentive love is a kind of experiential wisdom open to all parents and it can be rejected by parents of any social class.

Yet, there is another aspect of practical wisdom related to fostering growth that is more directly tied to social status. Parents with certain levels of education and resources undoubtedly use this knowledge to foster their children's growth in a way that less privileged or educated parents cannot. Here, I am not emphasizing differences in approaches to childrearing, but, instead, trying to highlight a more direct connection between knowledge and certain aspects of children's development. For example, another way that all parents are committed to fostering growth is through education. Regardless of social status, all parents in Lareau's study wanted their children to do well in school and valued the kind of opportunities that education would open up to them.[3] However, the parent's level of education and "social capital" had a direct correlation to how effective the parents were in helping their children succeed in this area.

In the Marshall family, Ms. Marshall's children just missed the cutoff for getting into the gifted classroom (one by only two points). Ms. Marshall not only understood the difference (pedagogically) it would make to her children to be in this other class, but also had the knowledge and resources to have her kids independently tested and then advocate for them to be included (Lareau 2003, 176). In contrast, Wendy Driver is in fourth grade but still can barely read at a first grade level. Her educational issues were noticed as early as the beginning of third grade, but she has yet to receive a full level of intervention from the school. While part of this is a difference in how comfortable parents are in making demands on the school, part of it also relates to the general education of the parents and their ability to fully understand the situation.

> Ms. Driver clearly does not have an *independent* understanding of the nature or degree of Wendy's limitations, perhaps because she is unfamiliar with the kind of terms the educators use to describe her daughter's needs (e.g., a limited "sight vocabulary," underdeveloped "language arts skills"). (Emphasis in original. Lareau 2003, 210)

This not only undermines Ms. Driver's ability to know what kind of resources she may be able to draw on to help her daughter, but also undermines her ability to effectively advocate for her daughter with the school. Toward the end of the fourth grade there is a disagreement between the main teacher and the special education intervention specialist about whether to hold Wendy back the following school year. Given her inability to fully understand the nature of her daughter's issues, this disagreement among the professionals leaves Ms. Driver flummoxed.

> Faced with contradictory information, Wendy's mother seems both bewildered and intimidated by the possibility that any intervention on her part might end up introducing more errors and delays in the process of getting the best education for Wendy. (Lareau 2003, 213)

Thus, a lack of education—in a more general sense—can inhibit the practical wisdom some parents need to foster growth.

As these examples show, all parents can have some kinds of practical wisdom in relation to fostering growth—namely some level of attentive love. Yet, there are also other kinds of knowledge that can directly influence how effectively parents can foster growth in other areas. The above example shows this discrepancy in relation to the common goal of educational success, but there are other areas where this can also be an issue. In another example, Lareau talks about how Ms. Driver was confused by the dentist using the language of both "cavity" and "tooth decay." She does not seem to understand that these are the same thing. In this way, a lack of vocabulary or certain kinds of education may limit parents' ability to foster growth in relation to healthy behaviors, understanding medical options, and access to resources.

Before moving on, let us briefly consider one other complication related to fostering development and the kind of practical wisdom it requires. A traditional goal for parents has been some level of independence for their children. What does this mean for parents whose children will never be able to take care of themselves? In *Love's Labor*, Eva Kittay discusses many aspects of raising a severely disabled child. Much of her analysis takes issue with the emphasis on independence and autonomy in theories of distributive justice; however, Kittay also considers the goals of parenting proposed by Ruddick.

For example, preservative love is often a more complex endeavor. Many disabilities come with a variety of medical issues that must be monitored and treated. As a result, disabled children are often more vulnerable. If the disability is severe enough, parents must face the reality that their child will never be capable of self-preservation. When this is the case, parents must figure out how to best secure long-term preservative care for their child. For those without resources, this is clearly a very difficult and sometimes impossible task.

Kittay also discusses the particular complications related to fostering development. Instead of focusing on independence, Kittay says that we should consider what capacities this specific child has and work toward enabling development of those. This will inevitably lead to a need for parents to advocate on behalf of their child. Parents will need to find appropriate resources (schools, teachers, medical personnel, etc.) that are relevant to their child's needs. Then the parents will have to work with these professionals to make sure the child is actually getting the care he or she needs—be this working on a specific treatment plan for occupational therapy or navigating an Individualized Education Plan (IEP) meeting with the child's school.

Although she does not use the language of virtue, Kittay also discusses specific parental skills that are necessary for fostering this development. Parents must become adept at navigating bureaucracies and negotiating with authority figures and institutions. For example, parents must work in conjunction with a number of professionals. The professionals bring expertise, but this expertise is generalized knowledge and narrow in focus. Consider an IEP meeting for an autistic child. The occupational therapist is an expert in how to help children with handwriting and will likely see improving handwriting as a necessary goal for academic success. In contrast, the parent brings to the meeting an expertise in her own child. This includes insight into how much frustration this child can handle in relation to this goal. The parent is also looking at the child more holistically. How does this educational goal fit with other educational goals? How much time can the family devote to hand exercises versus other necessary interventions? How do these academic goals relate to social goals or other needs of the child or family as a whole? In this way, parents must learn to negotiate with and coordinate between a variety of professionals on behalf of their child. Notice also how this favors the middle-class norms previously discussed. Working-class and poor parents will already be at a disadvantage—a disadvantage that is then passed on to their children.

Parents must also make some decisions about how much time and energy to give to a specific goal versus others. This leaves parents who are embroiled in these negotiations particularly vulnerable to self-doubt and guilt. Certainly, all parents will have moments of doubt and guilt, but, in addition to the normal kinds of parental guilt, these parents must ask additional questions: Am I doing enough for my child? Is this therapy/intervention the right choice? Knowing all the while that the wrong choice could make a significant difference in what the child is able to achieve. As Kittay says, "Some of these concerns are common to raising any child. But many of these concerns take on special poignancy when the very possibility of your child developing some fundamental skills to stay alive depend on your making the right decisions" (Kittay 1999, 171). For some, it could mean the difference between self-sufficiency (when this is an option) or not. On the flip side, parents of children with disabilities might also be subject to a unique kind of pride. When the latest intervention seems to be working and the child is making progress, parents can feel a sense of accomplishment. They rose to and met the challenge they were given and, as a result, for the time being, both they and their child are flourishing in some way.

SOCIAL ACCEPTANCE

The main goal of parents is to see their children into adulthood; however, most parents also hope to see their children flourish. To flourish in a given time and place, the child must also achieve some level of social acceptance. However, this particular goal is fraught with potential pitfalls. What if your child has character traits that would not automatically be undermining of her flourishing, but for the fact that society as a whole finds them socially unacceptable? Now the parent is faced with a dilemma—whether to intervene and try to change the child and, if so, how. There are a variety of ways this situation can occur—raising an introverted child in a world of extroverts, trying to teach social norms to a child on the autism spectrum, preparing a child to survive the oppressive norms of a racist society, or finding ways to keep a child safe in relation to the often violent response to those who do not conform to prevailing gender norms. Whenever there is something about a child that goes against the grain, a parent is faced with the decision of how to respond.

In her analysis of training, Ruddick focuses on how to approach this training (e.g., dominance versus what she calls educative control) and the problem of inauthenticity—"a repudiation of one's own perceptions and values" (Ruddick 1989, 112). While she does discuss the idea of reflecting on what values and norms the mother is trying to inculcate in her child, she does not have a sustained discussion of how a mother might go about making this decision. I offer some preliminary thoughts here.

As my previous examples show, there are many character traits that a particular society may find socially unacceptable that are not inherently detrimental to an individual's flourishing. In these cases, the parent will have to contemplate the need for social acceptance against the nature of the child. Is it the case that the child may find a sub-community in which she can flourish? In which case the parent may accept this trait and simply help the child develop survival skills and connect to the sub-community. Or, is it the case that this trait is so unacceptable that the child would face total ostracism and possibly death? In this case, the parent may be faced with a tragic dilemma. As Hursthouse explains a tragic dilemma is a kind of hard choice where the person cannot escape with clean hands.

> An action is right if it is what a virtuous agent would, characteristically, do in the circumstances, except for tragic dilemmas, in which a decision is right if it is what such an agent would decide, but the action decided upon may be too terrible to be called "right" or "good." (And a tragic dilemma is one from which a virtuous agent cannot emerge with her life unmarred.) (Hursthouse 2001, 79)

I would argue that a society that forces a parent to choose between allowing a child to express a key aspect of her character (that is not harmful to herself or others) and the safety/survival of her child is a society that presents a parent with a tragic dilemma. In these situations, the parent may be forced to curtail this trait in her child, but a loving parent would only do so with a heavy heart and, thus, would not escape with "clean hands." Also, it may not be possible to remove the undesired trait at all—for example, if you are living in a violently racist or misogynistic environment. In this case, the only option may be attempting to develop a protective sub-community and imparting other survival skills.[4]

We could say more about what we mean by flourishing and the pros/cons of survival with limited "flourishing." I address both these questions in more detail in subsequent chapters. My point here is simply to highlight how, training for social acceptance can potentially raise difficult questions that require the skills of practical wisdom and, in fact, bring up a new aspect of practical wisdom.

The skills articulated by Hursthouse and Swartwood tend to assume that we already have some goals or ends in mind—specifically, we have some knowledge of the virtues and are simply trying to "get it right" in enacting them. However, Ruddick's commitment of training for social acceptance raises questions about the ends/goals themselves. For an analysis of this aspect of practical wisdom, I return to the work of Monica Mueller. Her motivating question is how can we resist or at least question practices that are adopted by an entire culture yet are detrimental to groups of people within that culture? She ultimately argues that practical wisdom must include some deliberation on ends.

Aristotle makes clear that some kind of deliberation must be connected to practical wisdom. Mueller argues that this cannot *just* be deliberation on how to best achieve predetermined ends—this would be mere cleverness, which Aristotle argues is not the same thing as practical wisdom (*Nicomachean Ethics*, 1144a25–30).[5] So, what kind of deliberation must this be? Mueller emphasizes reflective endorsement of ends. In this way, we cannot simply adopt (intuitive) ends given by our culture because our culture and socialization can go wrong. On the other hand, we also cannot simply construct ends through abstract contemplation and then rigidly stick to them. There must be some engagement with the practical, real-world and other people (Mueller 2013, 21–22).

Mueller uses Arendt's discussion of the different view between spectators and actors to show how this kind of reflection might proceed. We sometimes take the view of a spectator—analyzing and judging another's action; other times we are the actors—too caught up in the moment of action to explicitly reflect on or think about our behavior. However, we can also take the spectator view in relation to our own past actions as a way to create an inner dialogue about our own actions and ends. Mueller, in keeping with Arendt, argues that, when doing this inner reflection, we should try to consider as many practical viewpoints as possible. In this way, we can think about how our actions would be viewed by others as well as our initial reaction to our own actions.

As Mueller argues, those who discuss practical wisdom tend to assume that the ends are given. I believe this is implied in the way that theorists tie wisdom and virtue without much discussion of how we settle on the specific virtues. However, Mueller claims that, if we think about the difference between *techne* and practical wisdom, we see that practical wisdom belongs to a more open-ended form of action. It is not strict ends/means action in the way *techne* is. This opens the possibility of reflection on ends. If we consider the relationship between spectator and action, we can see how this reflection takes place. Mueller also thinks there is room for reflection on ends within Aristotle's theory. Consider Aristotle's discussion of happiness—he opens the conversation by considering various understandings of happiness. In this way, he is inviting his students to reflect on this concept (end). Similarly, I can open a dialogue with myself about my previous actions. In this way, I open myself up for self-reflection during which I might reassess my actions or ends and, thereby, act differently in the future (Mueller 2013, 57–58).

Eventually, she ties this reflection back to the use of exemplars in learning and acting on virtue. Practical wisdom requires experiences with an exemplar and considering the role exemplar's play also helps identify the kind of knowledge involved.

> Looking to experience with an exemplar reveals the field of knowledge to which practical wisdom pertains, namely the spoken words and deeds of actors, people who live together in a shared common world. Becoming practically wise involves an analysis of the possibilities for human action and indicates the potential for human action at its best. (Mueller 2013, 44)

In the end, Mueller's main argument is that we create exemplars (especially through judgment on others' actions—as a spectator) that then become active when we recognize the particulars of a given situation to be a similar kind of thing. In this way, we use reflective thinking and judgment to choose ends (even though the endorsement happens earlier). This also leaves room for reevaluation of ends. In judging and deciding on exemplars, we will likely share our thoughts with others (Mueller 2013, 65). Indeed, she argues that in choosing exemplars we must take account of as many perspectives as possible (Mueller 2013, 78).

In this way, Mueller gives us a way to step back from ourselves and our culture and reflect on our actions or question the ends socialization has given us. This gives parents a way to reflect on the norms society tells them they should inculcate in their children and decide for themselves if this is really the best way to proceed. It also helps highlight another aspect of practical wisdom in relation to parenting. Depending on the norm and how it relates to her child's potential to flourish, this reflection may also lead a parent to work to change society instead of her child.

Parents of disabled children (and children with other "differences") also have a more complicated task when it comes to social acceptance. First, parents must learn to accept the child and her differences for themselves. For families who cannot come to terms with their child's disability or difference, it will be difficult or impossible for them to help their child navigate the perils of social acceptance. Second, and related, parents must find a balance between normalization and acceptance. By this I mean parents must figure out how much to try and change their child to better fit with the norms of society versus how much the parent should try to get society to accept the differences of their child. Kittay explains it this way:

> This socialization has two parts. First I refuse to see my child as not "normal"—for what she does is *normal for Sesha*. This is a redefining of normalcy that accepts Sesha in her individuality. Without such acceptance, I would not be able to present to the world a child *I* find acceptable. At the same time, I have to see the child as others see her so that I mediate between her and the others—to negotiate acceptability. The parental task involves then both socializing the child for acceptance, such as it might be, of the world, and socializing

the world, as best you can, so that it can accept your child. (Emphasis in original. Kittay 1999, 168–69)

This debate between "normalization" and acceptance has become particularly intense in recent debates over autism. Many in the autism community feel that there is nothing wrong with them and, thus, they should not be forced to adapt to "neurotypical" norms. Instead, they argue that autistics should be accepted as they are, and we should embrace the diversity and talents they bring to our community (Solomon 2008).

I take up the question of normalization versus acceptance in more detail in chapter 5. Here I only introduce it as a way to think about one aspect of parental wisdom. As we can see, reflecting on the goal of social acceptance requires all the previous skills related to practical wisdom and more.

In sum, I have outlined a number of ways our understanding of practical wisdom might relate to parenting. In our day-to-day activities, parents are confronted with a number of situations that require correct discernment, good comprehension, and good deliberation. If we take Ruddick's three main goals of parenting—preservation, fostering growth, and training for social acceptance—we see how many skills required for practical wisdom are relevant to parenthood. We also see forms of practical wisdom (such as embodied knowledge) and specific virtues (such as survival skills) that were not part of Aristotle's theory. In this way, we see the limits of Aristotle's original theory and how we must refine it to make it relevant to our contemporary society and sensibilities. I will continue this project in the next chapter as I take up a more sustained analysis of the concept of flourishing.

NOTES

1. The arguments I make in this chapter assume the child lives with the parent(s). For children who do not live with their parent(s), the situation is more complicated. The kind of practical wisdom discussed here may still be possible, but I will not give an in-depth analysis of that situation here.

2. Ruddick has specific reasons for using the maternal/mothering language. I recognize (and have some sympathy) with her reasons for this. However, I will be more fluid in my language and use parent, mother, and occasionally father.

3. Granted, depending on social status, the specific goals may vary (such as exact grades they expected or completing high school versus completing college). Still parents uniformly valued education and were interested in supporting their children's success in this area.

4. These dilemmas also raise questions about social activism and attempts to change the culture. I will say more about this in the next chapter.

5. Hursthouse also makes a similar point in her discussion of practical wisdom. The merely clever can use their skills for immoral ends. This is why the practically wise must also have virtue (Hursthouse 2006).

Chapter Three

Flourishing?

Raising Children in an Unjust Society

When I initially thought about this chapter, my goal was to think about the parental role in helping children flourish. Specifically, what can parents do to help facilitate their children's flourishing? Yet, when I started to map this out, I found the situation to be much more complicated. First, I think much of what parents can or cannot do to help children flourish has already been addressed in the previous two chapters. After all, those are the skills for developing a virtuous character that Aristotle claims is necessary for flourishing. Second, as Aristotle recognizes, there is a strong connection between the kind of society one lives in and an individual's ability to flourish. It is this second part that I will focus on in this chapter. Questions I will consider include: How do certain kinds of injustice undermine the connection between virtue and flourishing? How does this complicate the parental role? What responsibilities do parents of more privileged children have? Much of this discussion will take us beyond Aristotle's theory; however, I begin with a brief explanation of flourishing in relation to Aristotle's theory.

WHAT IS EUDAIMONIA?

Aristotle calls eudaimonia a kind of happiness. However, as many have documented, the Ancients' understanding of "happiness" is very different from our own (Annas 1993). To avoid confusion, my preferred translation is flourishing. According to Aristotle, eudaimonia is a kind of "excellence" that is "self-sufficient" and contributes to "living well." By self-sufficient he does not mean a kind of rugged individualism, but instead emphasizes the idea that this is an end goal (not something we do for something else). Ultimately, eudaimonia is a kind of living well. We have lived life the way we should—namely, as a virtuous person. Aristotle admits that we may still be plagued by misfortune (which ultimately diminishes the overall goodness of our life), but cultivating the virtues will always contribute to the goodness of our life (and help in our flourishing). Rosalind Hursthouse uses the following analogy. Suppose your physician recommends that you quit smoking and get more exercise. The physician is offering this as the best advice on how to be healthy. Suppose you do this, but still end up getting lung cancer. This does not mean that the physician gave you bad advice. This was a legitimate prescription for promoting health, it is just not a guarantee. Similarly, cultivating the virtues will not ensure flourishing, but they "are the only reliable bet" (Hursthouse 2001, 172). In sum, the virtues are necessary, but not sufficient.

Even with this general introduction, we are still left with many questions about what this successful life will look like. For Aristotle, it was a man of noble birth who had a good family and participated in politics and the contemplative life. Clearly, this is too narrow, anachronistic, and elitist for our current purposes. However, I will not attempt to give an alternate account here. I believe most parents have general goals for their children such as the ability to have significant relationships with others, to take care of themselves, and to have meaningful work or goals. Given our pluralistic society, I believe we can accept some subjectivity here.

Instead of giving a detailed account of what flourishing could be, I want to focus on the connection between virtues and flourishing or how an unjust society can corrupt the project of virtue theory. As many theorists have pointed out, Aristotle believed the state had a significant role in creating circumstances in which citizens could flourish. However, Aristotle had a very different vision of what a just state would look like. Given our modern understanding of human rights we need to modify Aristotle's theory such that it does not condone various kinds of domination.

In her book, *Burdened Virtues*, Lisa Tessman argues that feminist moral theory must account for flourishing (or the limits to flourishing) under oppression.

> The problem arises because of an assumption of his [Aristotle's] that I believe to be correct: that virtue is necessary but not sufficient for *eudaimonia* or flourishing. This fact creates a tension whenever those conditions that, in addition to virtue, are necessary for flourishing, are actually absent. (Emphasis in original. Tessman 2005, 159)

Specifically, she argues that we need to expand Aristotle's list of things that can interfere with flourishing to include systemic barriers of oppression. [1]

Ultimately, Tessman outlines a number of ways the systemic barriers of oppression can undermine flourishing. One, systemic injustice can rob some groups of the opportunity to develop certain virtues. Two, systemic injustice may skew what counts as a virtue. In other words, we may want to question whether some things an unjust society counts as virtues are really virtues and, similarly, whether everything considered a vice is truly a vice. Third, systemic injustice can skew virtues in an even more drastic way. Those living under situations of systemic oppression may be forced to develop what Tessman calls "burdened virtues." These are virtues only insofar as they contribute to survival, but, unlike traditional virtues, they do not contribute to flourishing in the normal sense. In what follows, I begin with a discussion of the first two problems Tessman identified; later, I take up the more significant problem of burdened virtues. Ultimately, I will discuss not only the problems faced by those who experience injustice, but also the responsibility those in a more privileged position have in working to remedy injustice.

PARENTING STYLES, SYSTEMIC INJUSTICE, AND FLOURISHING

Let us return to Annette Lareau's sociological research in *Unequal Childhoods*. Recall that Lareau identifies and analyzes two main parenting styles. Middle-class parents participate in what she calls "concerted cultivation." In this model, parents cultivate children's talents—specifically, linguistic and reasoning skills as well as any natural talents such as sports or music. Children are actively taught how to negotiate with authority figures to get what they need or want. As such, children grow up with a sense of entitlement and the skills necessary to succeed in their interactions with various bureaucracies and institutions. In contrast, working-class and poor parents approach parenting in a way that she calls "accomplishment of natural growth." These parents believe it is their duty to provide for basic needs (food, shelter, etc.), love their children, and set boundaries (i.e., appropriate discipline), which includes teaching their children right from wrong. If parents uphold these duties, they believe children will have what they need to grow into happy and successful adults. Unlike the middle-class parents, they do not see their children as "projects" in need of cultivating. Instead they are children who need a safe and nurturing space to enjoy childhood before they must take on the responsibilities of being an adult.

As Lareau points out, there are pros and cons to each of these approaches; however, our society encourages and rewards the skills learned in the concerted cultivation approach. Middle-class children learn verbal and reasoning skills that contribute to educational success. This success is not only reflected in grades and test scores, but also in attention and time. A student who shares stories about her challenges and successes in sports or other extra-curricular activities will be given more positive reinforcement than a child discussing his favorite television show. The middle-class children also learn how to interact and negotiate with authority figures and bureaucratic institutions. Their parents often intervene on their behalf and encourage them to practice negotiating for themselves. In contrast, working-class and poor children are taught to obey and not question authority. Similarly, their parents may interact with schools when called to do so, but rarely advocate on their child's behalf. This is not due to a lack of care. It is simply that most defer to the teacher's authority. They see it as the school's job to educate their children. Also, many fear the power schools have to call in social services and intervene in the family. In this way, middle-class children gain more "cultural capital" or "skills individuals inherit that can then be translated into different forms of value as they move through various institutions" (Lareau 2003, 7).

As we see from this brief sketch, the fact that society values the skills learned through concerted cultivation means these children have a better chance of flourishing in a general sense. They have better access to well-paying jobs, a wider variety of jobs and opportunities, social institutions better serve their needs, and society celebrates the kinds of virtues they exhibit. In contrast, working-class and poor children have a more circumscribed range of jobs which usually pay less, their interactions with institutions are often stilted if not hostile, and society denigrates many of the virtues they have cultivated. In sum, we see how society supports and rewards one parenting style over another.

Returning to Tessman, I would argue the discrepancy here relates to both a lack of opportunity to develop some virtues and a question about what counts as a virtue. Let us consider each of these in turn. First, Tessman argues that systemic barriers can influence our ability to develop virtues needed for flourishing.

> That is, in order to make progressive use of the linking of virtue to flourishing, one needs to assert that the underdevelopment of the virtues can itself have structural or systemic sources rather than, for instance, sources in what is inherent, biologically given, or simply accidental. *There is injustice already at work in the formation of character; the fact that something is based on character does not imply that it is not also rooted in an oppressive social system.* (Emphasis added. Tessman 2005, 36)

In this way, the deck is already stacked against certain groups. Consider the difference in educational achievement and the effect this has on job opportunities.

Many schools today are rated on what is called the achievement gap. This is generally assessed by comparing standardized test scores based on race and socioeconomic status. If kids in the same school show a significant difference based on these categories, then the school is said to have a significant achievement gap (and is admonished to do something about it). However, as many have pointed out, this is often the result of an opportunity gap that the school can only partially remedy. There are a list of things such as high quality preschool, access to enrichment activities, and even family trips that are known to help support the kind of academic achievement reflected in these test scores. As Lareau's study shows, these are the kinds of activities and experiences middle-class children have access to and we see the results—greater educational success (which usually leads to increased job opportunities).

In this way, we can see how systemic barriers lead some groups to have less opportunity to develop some of the virtues and this limits their overall flourishing. I should point out that this does not mean these groups cannot flourish at all. It is simply, as Tessman says, that the deck is stacked against them. However, as I mentioned earlier, there are pros and cons to both of the parenting styles identified by Lareau. With this in mind, I turn now to the second problem identified by Tessman.

In addition to looking at the development of specific virtues, Tessman also argues that we can question what *counts* as a virtue.

> It will also be important to realize that mainstream accounts of the virtues may be wrong in precisely the same way that status quo social arrangements corresponding to those virtues are wrong, and that therefore what are considered to be the virtues that subordinated people characteristically lack may not really be praiseworthy traits at all. (Tessman 2005, 48)

I believe we can question some of the virtues exhibited by middle-class children/parents. While the sense of entitlement may be useful in negotiating with institutions, it is not a universal good. For example, the children of working-class and poor parents tended to be much more respectful to adults while the middle-lass children often argued and whined. Also, Lareau points out that working-class and poor families tend to have much stronger family ties. Siblings fight less and the extended family is an integral part of their social circle and support network.

> In these areas, the lack of advantage is *not* connected to the intrinsic value of the McAllister family life or the use of directives at home. Indeed, one can argue that raising children who are polite and respectful and do not whine, needle, or badger their parents is a highly laudable child-rearing goal. Deep and abiding ties with kinship groups are also, one might further argue, important. Rather, *it is the specific ways that institutions function that ends up conveying advantages to middle-class children.* (Emphasis in original and added. Lareau 2003, 160)

Again, it is the way society ranks the virtues rather than something intrinsic in the virtues themselves that makes them qualify as a detriment to flourishing. Indeed, we might flourish more as a society if we all had stronger familial ties instead of cultivating the competitive, individualistic notion of success advocated in middle-class families.

To further clarify Tessman's second point, let us consider some specific outcomes of each parenting style that reflect skewed values. Even though the concerted cultivation of middle-class parenting is encouraged by society, research shows that some of the character traits developed may not be conducive to developing a virtuous character. For example, in one series of studies, those who would be categorized as lower-class were more compassionate and trusting (Piff et al. 2010). In another study, upper-class individuals had less empathy and were less able to recognize signs of distress in others (Kraus, Piff, and Keltner 2011). There is some disagreement about how much we should generalize based on these studies. However, if we return to our discussion of parenting styles, we see how these values *might* be cultivated through specific kinds of upbringing.

As we have seen, a major benefit of concerted cultivation is that it develops skills that are more likely to lead to economic success. All the extracurricular activities are not only to develop talents, but also to promote academic success. Much of this behavior is geared toward helping children get into a good college, which parents see as crucial for future economic success (Senior 2014, 144). Lareau points out that this also develops in children an individualistic and competitive nature. Children spend much of their time in competitive extra-curricular activities. This bleeds over into other aspects of their lives. Siblings are competitive and fight more. Birthday parties are often elaborate affairs and involve mostly children from school or extra-curricular activities. In contrast, working-class and poor children in her study often had stronger family ties. Siblings fought less, birthday parties were simpler and centered around family. These families often relied more on extended family members for various kinds of help and social support. Thus, we see how the day-to-day lives of children could lead to discrepancies in ethical behavior later in life.

While individualism, competitiveness, and an intense focus on goal-oriented behaviors may contribute to flourishing in the form of academic and economic success, they also have the potential to undermine our commitment to remedying some forms of injustice. For example, some studies show that those with more wealth are less likely to give to charity (Piff et al. 2010; Kraus, Piff, and Keltner 2011; Stern 2013). As one researcher who participated in these studies speculates, "the personal drive to accumulate wealth may be inconsistent with the idea of communal support" (Stern 2013). I will return to the problem of privilege and injustice later. I introduce it here as a way to critique the ordering of values we currently see and point out how that inhibits flourishing for both groups (albeit in different ways).

Many working-class and poor parents spend most of their time focused on meeting children's basic needs so they have little time or money left to organize and facilitate the kinds of enrichment activities that middle-class children enjoy. As we have seen, these enrichment activities are directly related to educational success, which ultimately promotes economic success. Thus, the unequal access to these goods undermines the opportunity some groups have to develop some virtues—namely, middle-class children have more opportunities to develop cultural capital. Indeed, we see this is a huge contributor to the "achievement gap" so we could argue that society has some responsibility to provide access to some of these experiences as a way to increase the range of opportunities available to *all* children.

THE BURDENS OF SYSTEMIC OPPRESSION

I initially outlined three problems Tessman identified that can create a dis-connect between virtue and flourishing: (1) lack of opportunity to develop some virtues, (2) injustice in how society categorizes virtue/vice, and (3) what Tessman calls "burdened virtues." The last section considered the first two, now I turn my attention to the third. The first problem—lack of opportu-nity—can largely be remedied by resources. The second and third problems require more than resources; they require envisioning alternative cultural values. As I mentioned, the values inculcated in middle-class children reflect our individualistic and competitive culture. However, our culture also has a deep history of racism, misogyny, and homophobia. These prejudices like-wise undermine flourishing in ways Aristotle did not address. In this section, I turn my attention to burdened virtues and systemic violence. The main example I draw on here is race.

Before we begin this discussion, I want to add a brief note about personal positioning. As a white, heterosexual woman, I am most prepared to speak on one narrow aspect of gender. Still, it would be irresponsible to write a chap-ter on parents and flourishing in the age of Black Lives Matter and ignore the systemic violence inflicted on black families. While I do not believe individ-uals must have personal experience to write about an issue, I do believe we must be careful not to speak for others. In order to try to avoid the arrogance of speaking for others, I will do my best to let black parents and theorists speak for themselves. Thus, I will draw my examples from the work they are already doing on this issue—while trying to show how it might inform the virtue theory analysis we are working on here.

According to Tessman, some virtues may be necessary for survival, but are not necessarily conducive to overall flourishing. These are what Tessman calls "burdened virtues."

> What I think of as the *burdened virtues* include all those traits that make a contribution to human flourishing—if they succeed in doing so at all—*only* because they enable survival of or resistance to oppression (it is in this that their nobility lies), while in other ways they detract from their bearer's well-being, in some cases so deeply that their bearer may be said to lead a wretched life. (Emphasis in original. Tessman 2005, 95)

Tessman focuses mainly on virtues or traits encouraged by activist communities. I will discuss survival skills passed on by parents. For example, Tamara Winfrey Harris discusses how the stereotype of Jezebel leads black parents to teach their daughters to suppress their sexuality. Consider the following quotes from women she interviewed:

> It's like: "I can't be that Jezebel. I can't be that Jezebel." We're so busy trying not to be Jezebel that we don't acknowledge our inner Jezebels and say that she's okay. That's the sad part.
>   I think [we're] taught from day one, you keep your legs closed and you're not supposed to desire sex and sex is something that you give away or that's taken from you or that's done to you. . . . We're not taught that sex is pleasurable. (Winfrey Harris 2015, 38)

Many parents feel the need to suppress their daughter's sexuality because the Jezebel stereotype has devastating real-life implications. It simultaneously makes black women more vulnerable to sexual assault, but also makes people less likely to believe black women's stories of being assaulted. Black women come to be seen as "unrapable." However, in trying to avoid this stereotype women are taught to deny and suppress their own sexuality. This would certainly count as a burdened virtue.

The definition Tessman is working with seems to be very narrowly tailored—the burdened virtue's *only* relationship to flourishing is that it enables survival or resistance. However, there are also virtues to which many have a more ambiguous relationship—such as the stereotype of the strong black woman. Surveys of black women find mixed reactions to this stereotype. Some find a kind of strength in it that helps them feel more confident and builds self-esteem. Yet, most also admit that it can undermine women's ability to care for themselves and often leads others to ignore the complexity of their humanity. After all, "strong" women do not need help. Again, we can see this ambivalence in how some women approach the lessons they want to teach their daughters:

> I am raising a daughter. The reality is, a certain kind of strength will be required for her to make it through this life with her sanity and health—to not let racism and sexism kill her. But I have to be very careful about telling her to be strong, because I also want her to be fully human. (Winfrey Harris 2015, 100)

In these examples, we see how raising children under oppression can distort the project of virtue theory. It can require teaching what Tessman has called "burdened virtues" or virtues that do not inherently promote flourishing, but are necessary for survival.

In the wake of discussions related to police violence, we see another burdened virtue. The rest of society is now aware of how black parents must decide when and how to give their children "the talk"—an explanation of police violence and strategies to try to minimize the potential for escalation. As Ta-Nehisi Coates tells his son:

> You are a black boy, and you must be responsible for your body in a way that other boys cannot know. Indeed, you must be responsible for the worst actions of other black bodies, which, somehow, will always be assigned to you. And you must be responsible for the bodies of the powerful—the policeman who cracks you with a nightstick will quickly find his excuse in your furtive movements. And this is not reducible to just you—the women around you must be responsible for their bodies in a way that you never will know. (Coates 2015, 71)

Here we see how the realities of systemic violence lead black parents to teach their children that they must self-police their behaviors in ways that white children do not have to worry about.

While I am focusing here mainly on the issue of racial violence, we see a similar self-policing and training of women in relation to sexual violence.

> Women in the modern world have trained, to the point of unconscious reflex, for encounters with potential male threat, discomfort, or annoyance. We carry our keys between our fingers on late nights. We wear headphones with the sound off to hear if we're being followed. We get into another train car if the closest one is full of drunk men. We monitor our smiles, arm positions, bodies and words: *I don't want to give him the wrong idea. Please don't come near me. Please don't get offended. Please don't assume that my politeness means I'm flirting. Please regard me professionally. Please leave me alone.* (Thorpe 2017)

Our previous discussion of the Jezebel stereotype shows how this problem is even more difficult for black women to navigate.

To fully understand the toll systemic racial violence takes, we must also understand its deep history and how young these lessons start. From slavery to lynching to the civil rights era to today, black families have had to contend with this threat. Discussing her youth in the Jim Crow south, bell hooks explains:

> I grew up in the apartheid South. We learned when we were very little that black people could die from feeling rage and expressing it to the wrong white folks. We learned to choke down our rage. This process of repression was aided by the existence of our separate neighborhoods. In all black schools, churches, juke joints, etc., we granted ourselves the luxury of forgetfulness. (hooks 1995, 13)

As hooks points out, this training often begins very young and parents today still feel the pull to start this training very early. Coates tells a story of visiting a preschool and his family is invited to tour a gym where all the children are playing. His son exuberantly joins the crowd—unafraid and uninhibited. Coates's initial reaction is to pull his son back and instruct him to police his behavior given that these are strangers and there is no telling what their reaction will be. However, Coates does not do this. Instead he holds himself back and reflects on the nature of this burdened virtue:

> But now I understand the gravity of what I was proposing—that a four-year-old child be watchful, prudent, and shrewd, that I curtail your happiness, that you submit to a loss of time. And now when I measure this fear against the boldness that the masters of the galaxy imparted to their own children, I am ashamed. (Coates 2015, 92)

Here we can see how burdened virtues undermine flourishing for both children and parents. For parents, it complicates the parental projects of fostering development and preservative love (discussed in the previous chapter). For children, the self-policing is not just a double standard, but also works against other aspects of virtue theory.

In thinking about how this kind of self-policing works against other virtues, we could initially point out how it makes the learning and expression of other-regarding virtues more fraught. There is an additional complexity or barrier that must be navigated. However, we can also think about this in another way. Using pragmatism to think about virtue theory, Jennifer Welchman argues that there are specific "minor" virtues associated with childhood. Her proposed list includes curiosity, playfulness, confidence, sympathy, trust, gratitude, and loyalty (Gardiner 2005). We can see how the self-policing behavior Coates is tempted to impose upon his son undermines all of these. Thus, we can see how the project of fostering development is more complicated for those raising children subject to systemic violence.

It also makes the project of preservative love more difficult and precarious. When violence is a form of oppression, it is visited upon the individual *based on group membership* (Young 1990). Part of what makes it oppressive is that the individual cannot avoid or escape the *threat* of violence. This also takes a toll on parents who know their children (as well as themselves) must live with this constant threat. Again, Coates felt the full weight of this after the birth of his son.

> Now at night, I held you and a great fear, wide as all our American genera-tions, took me. Now I personally understood my father and the old mantra—"Either I can beat him or the police." I understood it all—the cable wires, the extension cords, the ritual switch. Black people love their children with a kind of obsession. You are all we have, and you come to us endangered. I think we would like to kill you ourselves before seeing you killed by the streets that America made. (Coates 2015, 82)

Even though parents teach these survival skills, they may or may not be effective. It is impossible for a parent to fully protect a child from systemic violence.

All of this shows how oppression in the form of violence creates signifi-cant barriers to flourishing. Unfortunately, many groups are subject to sys-temic violence related to oppression—sexual and domestic violence perpe-trated against women, hate crimes against homosexuals and gender noncon-forming groups, and the long history of violence against black bodies and other people of color. As Black Lives Matter has made clear, this is a serious threat to the black community and the black family.

We also, again, see the disconnect between virtue and flourishing as it is traditionally understood in virtue theory. Aristotle believed virtues would always be conducive to flourishing and, furthermore, would count as a boon to those who suffered significant "bad luck." Aristotle also believed the "wicked" would not (could not?) flourish. While I doubt many of our current public leaders are drawing explicitly on Aristotle's theory, we hear an echo of this kind of thinking in the politics of respectability rhetoric.

Many argue that the black community could fix the problems of poverty, crime, violence, and so forth if they adopted the "appropriate" values. These are generally explained as character traits such as self-discipline, an appreci-ation for education and hard work, and a commitment to norms associated with the heterosexual nuclear family. Many would also fall under the kinds of virtues promoted by traditional virtue theory. In this reasoning, we see another injustice—being told it is your own character flaws instead of a corrupt system that is responsible for your lack of flourishing. This kind of rhetoric creates another burden to carry and allows society to ignore injus-tices that could be remedied.

We see how this creeps into the debate over systemic violence when victims are blamed for the violence perpetrated against them. We have seen this for years in discussions of rape and sexual violence. We also see this in debates over the epidemic of police violence brought to national attention by the Black Lives Matter movement. Every time there is a new case, the immediate response is to scrutinize the victim. What did he or she do? Could he or she have behaved in a way that avoided conflict? Or the immediate incident is ignored and instead the media focuses on a debate over the individuals' perceived character flaws. Did he steal from that convenience store? Why did she refuse to put her cigarette out? Yet, research shows this is a distraction. No amount of personal virtue can save an individual from systemic violence. Perhaps no case illustrates this better than the murder of Jordan Edwards.

Jordan Edwards and his family are an example of all the virtues those in the politics of respectability would expect. His parents are married, have good paying jobs, and are raising their children in a nice, middle-class neighborhood. Jordan Edwards had a 4.0 grade point average and played on his high school football team. He and his brothers were all scholar athletes. They also looked out for each other. One night, Jordan and his brothers went to a party. When the party became too crowded and rowdy, they decided to leave. Unfortunately, as they were leaving the party, they encountered the local police. While the boys were driving away, police shot and killed Jordan Edwards. After this, they harassed and arrested his brothers. When the officers could not find any charges to bring against them, the brothers were eventually released. As this case shows, a virtuous character is no protection against systemic racism (King 2017).

I raise this issue to show how a kind of echo of Aristotle haunts our current political debates. Here we see the idea that virtue is necessary for flourishing turned the other way to argue that those who do not flourish must not have virtue. In this way, they are responsible for their inability to flourish and, more precisely, their own "bad luck." This is only effective if we ignore the systemic issues that undermine flourishing. Thus, we have yet another reason to revise Aristotle's theory in a way that accounts for systemic barriers to flourishing.

THE RESPONSIBILITIES AND PITFALLS OF PRIVILEGE

We have been discussing systemic violence and the burdened virtues groups often adopt in response to this violence. However, the only way to "fix" this problem is to fix society itself. To do this, we need to change the structures that perpetuate it. We know that oppression is a systemic problem and cannot be fixed by any one individual. However, it is also the case that nothing will change until those in power recognize the problem and begin to work for change. With that in mind, I consider what special responsibilities parents who are raising children in the dominant group face. We could talk about a variety of dominant groups—heterosexuals, men, Christians, and so forth.

However, in response to our last section, I will focus mainly on raising white children in a racially unjust society.

According to Aristotle, the state has a role to play in creating the conditions in which citizens can flourish; however, Aristotle also endorsed various kinds of domination. As Tessman points out, Aristotle believed in treating equals equally and unequals unequally, but he had a very different idea of who counted as equals than we do today (Tessman 2005, 75). As a result his conception of flourishing is compatible with what we now call oppression. To remedy this, Tessman adds a kind of "addendum" to Aristotle's theory to say that "the health of a social collectivity" must be expanded beyond my own social group and the people I personally depend on. She adds a constraint on eudaimonistic goals to say they must also include the goals of liberatory politics. I agree with Tessman but, like her, I will not give a fully developed theoretical argument for this position. I consider what follows a beginning conversation that I invite others to build on.

Thinking specifically about the problem of racial injustice in the current United States, I will argue that white parents have a responsibility to raise their children to be antiracist. We can justify this using the following aspects of Aristotle's theory. First, promoting justice or being just is clearly a virtue. Given our modern understanding of equality and human rights racism is a form of injustice. As we will see in the following discussion, in a racist society, white people benefit from racism. As such, if I want to practice the virtue of justice I need to work to dismantle a system that unfairly bestows privilege on me at the expense of others. If I do not, I am complicit—and therefore perpetuating injustice. However, this is not the only reason white people should take up this cause. Second, and related, growing up in a white supremacist society skews our moral perception. Recall from chapter 1, the practical wisdom necessary for justice requires veridical moral perception or recognizing the morally salient features of the situation. This relates to the "good comprehension" aspects of practical wisdom discussed in chapter 2. In order to act virtuously, I need to understand what kind of situation I am faced with. Being socialized in a culture that supports and perpetuates racism undermines our ability to cultivate veridical moral perception in white children. It is this second point that I will focus on here. Current theories of race and race relations show that simply growing up white in our current culture can undermine the kind of practical wisdom necessary for racial justice (to take one example of liberatory politics). In the rest of this section, I will explain how this is the case and what parents can do about it.

To be fair, much of what I will discuss here goes beyond idiosyncratic parenting styles. It is simply the result of growing up in a culture that supports white supremacy in a variety of subtle and not so subtle ways. For example, growing up in a culture where your race is considered the norm against which all others are compared—indeed your "race" is so normalized

that you are not seen as having a "race" at all. You also see yourself repre-
sented in all aspects of society—politics, teachers, popular culture, and so
on.[2] In this way, all who consider themselves white will absorb these messages regardless of class or parenting styles. However, later I will discuss
some ways parents can work to counteract these influences. First, let us
revisit the process of instilling virtue and how it goes awry in this situation.

Recall our analysis of moral development in the first chapter. Through
habituation, we develop children's empathic abilities. However, both Aristotle and moral psychologists tell us this is a complicated process that involves
both affective and cognitive components. So, we cannot just work to make
children "feel bad" for what they have done and want to make it right, we
must also—as Sherman explains—cultivate children's powers of critical discernment. In this way, children learn to recognize the morally salient features
of what is happening. As children grow, hopefully so do their powers of
discernment. Practicing this skill helps children to develop what Gibbs calls
veridical moral perception—that is, they are able to recognize the salient
moral features of a situation even when there are distracting influences. In
the discussion that follows, these "distracting influences" might be cultural
messages and beliefs or peer groups that do not share the same understanding
of race and racial justice. Ideally, this practice of discernment combined with
experience and general cognitive development eventually leads to practical
wisdom. These were the key aspects of moral development outlined in chapter 1.

So what happens to this process if you are a white child growing up in a
racially unjust society? In what follows, I will make a variety of generalizations about white people. As the studies I draw on show, white people are not
used to having these kinds of generalizations made about them and many
may find my language off-putting or offensive. I would first ask that those
readers sit with and consider those emotional reactions in relation to the
arguments made here. However, I would also remind the reader that generalizations are just that—generalizations. I acknowledge that there is a significant and vocal subgroup of white people who are actively antiracist and
working to undo the attitudes discussed here. However, there is also a range
of literature that supports the generalizations I make here.[3]

In "White Woman Feminist," Marilyn Frye discusses a variety of traits
white people often passively develop from growing up in a white supremacist culture. She argues that these traits are similar to gender traits—they are
learned from society and, thus, can be undone, but only with much difficulty.
Also, like gender norms, these traits (and the implicit beliefs, norms, and
values associated with them) can often work on an unconscious level. In this
way, they can affect our judgment and behavior in ways we are not aware of
(Valian 1998). Continuing the analogy with feminine and masculine traits,
Frye calls these traits "whiteliness." For example, drawing on the work of

Minnie Bruce Pratt, she talks about how whites are taught to be judges—"a judge of responsibility and punishment, according to an ethical system which countenances no rivals" (Frye 1992, 153). In addition, white people—in general—also have "a staggering faith in their own rightness and goodness" (Frye 1992, 154) and a "belief in one's authority in matters practical, moral and intellectual" (Frye 1992, 156). Together, these traits create a toxic mix that inhibits white peoples' ability to accurately see injustice and, thus, inhibits our (collective as well as personal) ability to "be just."

If we return to our understanding of practical wisdom, we might say that what is needed is more knowledge—specifically, real world experiential knowledge that includes the perspective of others. Unfortunately, the traits inculcated as part of being white in the United States undermine a white person's ability to accurately discern the relevant aspects of an experience. Recall from chapter 1 that experiential knowledge can help develop veridical moral perception or being able to see the morally salient factors despite distracting influences. In a picture, the distracting influence would be the other geometrical shapes. In the example of the kid raised with racist views, the distracting influences were his peer group (as well as other cultural influences). Here the distracting influences are the traits of "whiteliness" and research shows they affect many whites—even those who do not hold explicitly racist views. Unfortunately, these distracting influences also undermine a white person's ability to gain experiential knowledge from personal discussion and perspective taking.

If we want to develop the practical wisdom necessary for the virtue of justice, white people need to be able to have productive conversations about race and the ability to understand very different experiences from their own; however, when it comes to race, white people are not good at having this kind of dialogue or learning from it. In her article on white fragility, Robin DiAngelo summarizes why white people find these conversations so difficult. Given that they often lead fairly segregated lives and are not taught to see themselves as having a race (which means race is not an issue they must concern themselves with), DiAngelo argues that white people are insulated from "race-based stress." As such, any conversation that makes them uncomfortable or challenges their view of themselves (see the characteristics previously discussed) triggers a defensive response.

> White Fragility is a state in which even a minimum amount of racial stress becomes intolerable, triggering a range of defensive moves. These moves include the outward display of emotions such as anger, fear, and guilt, and behaviors such as argumentation, silence, and leaving the stress-inducing situation. These behaviors, in turn, function to reinstate white racial equilibrium. (DiAngelo 2011, 54)

Thus, white people are often incapable of even hearing—let alone learning from—other's perspectives on racial issues. In chapter 1, we learned that empathy included biological, affective, and cognitive components. Here we see how learned aspects of whiteliness can cause cognitive, affective, and even biological responses that shut down empathy and, thus, inhibit productive dialogue from taking place.

To summarize the problem, let us return to Aristotle and his argument that a person needs to cultivate the right attitude in order to be prepared for certain learning. Specifically, Aristotle claims that reason and information are not enough. To be able to study and learn ethics one must first cultivate the right attitude toward the subject matter and what he hopes to learn. In this section, we see how growing up white in the United States inculcates certain personality traits and habituates certain defensive behaviors that are counterproductive to gaining the kind of experiential knowledge necessary for practical wisdom—at least in relation to racial justice. These beliefs and behaviors undermine dialogue and veridical moral perception—which derails a potential source of knowledge—which ultimately weakens the ability to understand and express justice. In sum, whites end up with poor skills of discernment, which are necessary for practical wisdom (which is necessary for virtue). I have focused on justice here, but we could also refer back to earlier discussion about compassion and generosity (or look at additional "other-oriented" virtues). We could also do a similar analysis in relation to other types of privilege versus systemic oppression. While being a member of an oppressed group encourages the development of double-consciousness,[4] being a member of a privileged group allows one to maintain a kind of ignorance and obliviousness to the experiences and perspectives of others. Much like Aristotle's students need the correct preparation (namely an upbringing that makes one want to be virtuous and take pleasure in virtuous things) to study ethics, white children need the correct preparation through upbringing that allows one to understand and work toward racial justice.

So, what's a parent to do? Fortunately, there are a number of things parents of privileged children can do to counteract these influences. The first thing we need to do is to understand the stages of racial identity development—as explained in Jennifer Harvey's *Raising White Kids*.[5] Much like theories of moral development, these "stages" are not mutually exclusive or strictly linear. However, they are a helpful tool for thinking about how we develop a racial identity and how that development shapes our understanding of and interaction with the world. To facilitate our current discussion, I give a brief overview of the stages, then discuss how this framework can help us think about raising antiracist children.

In the first stage, "contact," we believe everything is fine. We have a simple belief in equality and sameness. We see race as a positive thing, but also not a big deal—because we are all basically the same. More importantly, we believe we are all *treated* more or less the same. This is our general framework for interacting with the world. I need to be clear that there are two problems with this stage that will be relevant to our discussion. The first problem is that whites in the contact stage do not see racism as a significant problem. They believe society treats everyone as equals regardless of race and that instances when this is not the case are exceptions to the general rule. This is why they consider race to be no big deal. Many who are in this stage argue that we should promote "color-blindness"—which leads to our second (and related) problem.

In an ideal world, it would be great to cultivate a tendency to not see or discuss race. However, we do not live in an ideal world. Race is a salient issue in the day-to-day lives of all people whether they recognize it or not. So we need to teach children how to discuss these issues in a productive way. Unfortunately, admonishing children to be "color-blind" does the opposite. Noticing and discussing race or the effects of race are seen as taboo topics that one should avoid. It also causes a form of cognitive dissonance because children see the effect of race whether we acknowledge it or not:

> Color-blind teaching presents as an aspiration ("don't see it!") a charge that is fundamentally out of synch with their daily experience ("I see it every-where!"). In doing so, it actively distorts children's engagement with and interpretation of reality. When we teach an approach to race that fundamental-ly clashes with children's actual experiences and emerging knowledge, we are active participants in this distortion. (Harvey 2018, 38)

Therefore, if we want to raise white children to be antiracist, we need to help them process what they see in their day-to-day life. This will include learning how to have productive conversations about race rather than ignoring it.

The next stage, "disintegration," comes when this rosy picture of the world is shattered. Something happens that makes it impossible for us to ignore the prevalence of racism and the moral dilemmas that come with that recognition. Our original interpretive framework has been shattered, which creates stress. We need interpretive frameworks to navigate our world and, in an effort to reestablish a workable framework, we have two options.

The first option is "reintegration" or integrating our new knowledge (poor treatment of people of color) into our old framework (everything is fine). However, the only way to make this work is to blame people of color. If everything is fine but black people are treated poorly, then it must be their own fault (i.e., the politics of respectability). In this stage, the person may still be friends with some people of color—the "exceptional ones." Also, the person may not be explicitly racist—that is he or she may not adopt an explicitly white supremacist stance—but the white person will still internal-ize white superiority on some level. They would almost have to in order to makes sense of a framework that sees white people constantly in the privileged position, but wants to believe this is not the result of racism or racist social structures.

The second option is "pseudo-independence" and it is the beginning stage of developing a new interpretive framework. In this stage, the white person accepts the belief that there is something wrong with society and begins the work of building a new interpretive framework that helps makes sense of this fact. As Harvey summarizes, a person becomes "motivated to better understand what's actually going on and to learn about structural racism and how it functions" (Harvey 2018, 112). In this way, there is room for growth, but this is also a stressful stage and there is always the possibility of regression. This is because if we fully accept the reality of racism, we must also realize the role whites have played (and continue to play) in perpetuating this system. This leads to white guilt and fear. White guilt is a normal reaction to learning about the role whites have played in creating this system and how we continue to reap privileges in relation to it. However, white guilt is also unproductive in combating racism. So, whites need to move beyond this stage and develop a more useful relationship to their own whiteness. Once we realize the extent of racism and how it shapes us and society, this awareness brings fear of saying the wrong thing or "messing up." Becoming more comfortable with our own race and what it means also helps alleviate fear.

Fortunately, it is possible to move out of this stage and into a more productive place to do antiracist work. This stage is called "immersion." In addition to learning about racism, white people in the previous stage can also explore their own racial identity and what it means to be white. This awareness can lead to a new understanding of how I want to be white in the world. "I come to realize that I have the ability to *impact and challenge* the power of racism in my life and can participate in antiracist resistance to it" (Emphasis in original. Harvey 2018, 117). This realization allows white people to move past white guilt and fear. They may develop a "healthy moral anger." They also learn that they probably will mess up, but they can accept responsibility for that and move on. The commitment to antiracist work becomes stronger and white people realize they have a stake in racial justice above and beyond "helping" black people: "White supremacy malforms my humanity, constrains my life, compromises my spirit. When I recognize this I begin to see the fight against racism as also a life-giving struggle for my own liberation" (Harvey 2018, 119). At this point, we can really start to see the relationship to virtue theory and the need to cultivate a virtuous character.

The final stage is a kind of settling into many of the things learned in the immersion stage. As we achieve the "autonomy" stage, we realize that this will be an ongoing process. As such, we embrace the journey that will include continuing to learn and better ourselves. We become more confident in our ability to act, accept criticism, and recognize the need to stay accountable for our actions.

So what does this tell us about how to cultivate a virtuous character in white children? The first thing we should notice is that we cannot and should not ignore the issue of race. The standard approach for well-meaning whites has been to cultivate a "colorblind" perspective. We teach kids that we should not "see" race. Unfortunately, this creates a false interpretive framework. Kids will see in their day-to-day lives that race does matter. At best, they learn to avoid seeing or discussing race by ignoring these significant experiences in their lives. At worst, they are confronted with irrefutable facts that make it impossible to ignore racism and, thus, throws them into the disintegration stage. However, if we continue to ignore their distress (and the facts of the world), it will be difficult, if not impossible, for children to move on to the pseudo-independent stage. Instead, we make it more likely they will regress by either ignoring the initial information and slipping back into the contact stage or adopting some version of the reintegration stage.

Intuitively, the earlier we have these conversations, the easier these early transitions will be. Those of us who spent many years with the contact stage view of the world are likely to experience even more distress at having that interpretive framework shattered. In contrast, if children are introduced to the issue in developmentally appropriate ways at a young age, we can also help guide them through the stages of pseudo-independence and into immersion/ autonomy. Let us consider a couple practical examples of how this helps.

Recall that the pseudo-independence stage is often characterized by white guilt and fear. Harvey points out that this can be especially difficult for children. Many progressive and well-meaning schools work to promote diversity—by which they mean an embracing of various cultures and beliefs. However, this leaves white children in a difficult position. For obvious reasons, we cannot encourage white children to unreflectively "celebrate" being white. Harvey discusses how we can help white children feel less shame and "outsider" feelings in this situation by discussing our own histories of resistance. We cannot erase the history of white domination and oppression, but there have also almost always been individuals or groups working against that domination and oppression. Recognizing those figures in our history can help mediate the white guilt and shame that often accompanies studying the history of racism. It also gives white children role models and invites them to think about how they can contribute to the project of undoing racism. Using the language from our earlier discussion, we might explain the difference in approach like this. In the traditional "whitewashed" version of history, white children will learn various traits of "whiteliness." In contrast, *if* we study a more realistic version of our racial history—but one that also includes whites who resisted or fought against racism, then we give white children more tools for thinking about how they want to be white in the world (see discussion of immersion).

Another tool for working against the traits of whiteliness is to work toward "decentering" whiteness. In school, this could include studying a more robust version of history—one that includes stories of heroes of color beyond the token discussions in February. As parents, we can make an effort to expose our children to books, movies, and toys that have people of color in leading roles. This decentering works to create a more realistic diversity instead of a default norm that acknowledges others.

We also need to give children the tools and ability to discuss race. Our current approach shuts down these conversations. Not only does this lead to an avoidance of race and racial issues (see earlier discussion of white fragility), but it leads to other problems as well. We have been talking mostly in this section about justice, but avoiding the issue of race in favor of colorblindness undermines other virtues as well. For example, Aristotle spends a significant amount of time in the *Nicomachean Ethics* discussing the importance of friendships. Adopting a "colorblind" approach undermines our ability to nurture and maintain interracial friendships.

In these same well-meaning schools that promote diversity, we see lots of interracial friendships when children are young, but as children get older, it is more and more common for them to self-segregate into their own groups. Why does this happen? Harvey argues that a big reason for this is the fact that white children are incapable of having discussions about race.

> In fact, the difficulty of cross-racial friendships—a near impossibility if the white partner in the friendship doesn't understand race—is one reason teaching children to value diversity or even making sure white children experience diverse contexts as they grow does not solve the problem of how to raise white kids. There are serious benefits to experiencing diversity early in life for raising antiracist white children. But if parents don't take up discussions of race and racism explicitly with children, they are unlikely to succeed in remaining good friends to children of color over time. (Harvey 2018, 41)

As the children of color get older, they realize more and more how race plays a role in their lives. Yet, they cannot discuss this significant part of their day-to-day experience with their white friends. Instead they gravitate toward groups that understand this relevance and allow them to acknowledge and discuss it.

In relation to our earlier discussion of stages, white children in the contact stage cannot participate in discussions of race or acknowledge its significance in the way their black friends would need them to understand. If your day-to-day experience reinforces the reality of racism and your friend cannot acknowledge this, it is difficult to maintain that friendship. If white children are going to be able to maintain these friendships, they need to move into the immersion stage.

In a way, we have now come full circle. If we want white children to be able to gain the kind of experiential knowledge necessary for practical wisdom, they need to be able to have conversations about race. Learning to be comfortable with these conversations will also enable children at mixed-race schools to better maintain friendships as they get older. Maintaining these relationships has a number of positive benefits. In addition to the epistemological benefits for white children, it works to undermine the kinds of self-segregation that are perpetuated in our adult lives. Despite laws against *de jure* segregation, we remain a largely segregated society. This often leads to a variety of injustices. So undermining this trend will also be one more step in working toward a more just society.

NOTES

1. Please note that I use "oppression" here as it is defined in a number of feminist theories. Some key aspects include that it must apply to a person based on membership in a social group. It is also enforced via social structures—it is systemic in nature. In sum, the group experiences a variety of injustices based on membership in that group. Here is a small sampling of sources that help to further define this concept (Frye 1983; Young 1990; Bartky 1990).

2. I cannot give a full account of the ways the United States supports white supremacy and how this is incorporated into white identity. A full list of resources would also be quite long. For some explanation see (Mills 1997; Taylor 2003).

3. Here is a sampling of sources that support the kinds of claims I will make in the following argument: (DiAngelo 2011; Frye 1992; Harvey 2018; Helms 2000; Tatum 1997).

4. Double-consciousness is a kind of internal duality. Those who live under oppression must, as a matter of survival, know how those with more power view the world. As such, they always carry around the Other's view of themselves as well as their own view of themselves (and the world).

5. Harvey's discussion of racial identify formation (and the specific stages discussed here) is building on the work of Janet Helm's *A Race is a Nice Thing to Have: A Guide to Being a White Person or Understanding the White Persons in Your Life*. My discussion and suggestions are mainly inspired by Harvey's work.

Part II

Parental Virtues

Chapter Four

On the Immorality of Lying to Children about Their Origins

For centuries families have struggled with the question of whether or not to tell adopted children about their biological parents.[1] Currently, parents are encouraged to be honest with children and open-adoption is becoming more popular (for example, see Bartholet 1993; Benkov 1994). With the rise of assisted-reproductive technology and the use of "donor" gametes, we are again struggling with the question of whether children should be informed about their genetic parents. Similar to adoption, the trend in "donor" conceptions has been a move toward honesty and openness.[2] For example, the American Society of Reproductive Medicine's most recent Committee Opinion on this topic "strongly encourages" parents to be honest with children about using "donor" gametes (Daar et al. 2018). In response to this trend in everyday practice, I give a theoretical argument in favor of honesty. Using the moral work on trust and lying, I argue that allowing or encouraging children to believe you are their biological parent when you are not is a breach of trust in the parent-child relationship.

Many bioethical discussions focus on empirical harms such as a lack of medical history (McGee, Brakman, and Gurmankin 2001). Here I make a different kind of moral argument—specifically I want to argue that it is immoral to lie to children about their genetic origins regardless of whether any particular child is harmed. In other words, my argument does not rely on empirical evidence of specific harm or a utilitarian calculus of benefits and burdens. In contrast to arguments based on harm, others focus on the rights of the child especially as stated in the Universal Declaration of Human Rights (Firth 2001). While I find these approaches more compelling, I am also not making a rights-based argument. Instead, I make a virtue theory argument based on our understanding of trust, lies, and the nature of the parent-child relationship.

My argument draws heavily on Nancy Potter's *How Can I be Trusted?* While Potter emphasizes how social institutions encourage or undermine our ability to be a trustworthy person, I use her virtue theory of trustworthiness to consider the nature of trust in the parent-child relationship and what this means for being a trustworthy parent. In addition to developing a virtue theory of trustworthiness, Potter also pays significant attention to unequal power relations and the potential for exploitation—which will be important in our discussion of the parent-child relationship.

TRUST AND A TRUSTWORTHY CHARACTER

Before getting into the specifics of my argument, I would like to point out that this entire debate is an exercise in heterosexual privilege. Gay and lesbian couples routinely use "donor" gametes to create families. However, they do not have the option of lying to children about the nature of their origins. In what follows, I argue that heterosexual couples should resist the temptation to use this privilege in favor of making themselves more trustworthy parents.

Philosophical analyses of trust show it to be a relational and limited concept. Building on Annette Baier's theory, Potter defines trust in the following way:

> Trusting another involves an expectation or belief that the trusted person has good intentions with regard to the care of something we value and the ability to carry through with what is expected of him or her. This definition of trust directs us toward an understanding of its *relational* nature: when we trust others, we stand in a particular relation to them with regard to some good which we are entrusting to their care. Furthermore, this relation is one of vulnerability. Trust itself alters power positions (Baier 1986, 240): trusting others involves depending on them, being vulnerable to the possibility of disappointment or betrayal, and risking harm to self. This further feature of trust, in turn, indicates a moral requirement of the one *being trusted*: being worthy of another's trust requires that one takes care to ensure that one does not exploit the potential power that one has to do harm to the trusting person. (Emphasis in original. Potter 2002, 9–10)

Potter's definition highlights three aspects of the trusting relationship that will be important for my initial discussion of trust in the parent-child relationship. First, trust is a relational concept. We trust different people with different things and in different ways; therefore, we must pay attention to the specific relationship to understand the nature of trust and trustworthiness. Obviously, children trust parents to do many things. I highlight this when I discuss the changing nature of the relationship. However, in relation to our current dilemma, I will argue that in the parent-child relationship, children trust that parents will be accurate guides in learning about social categories and social relationships. Therefore, deception in relation to these categories is a breach of trust—regardless of good intentions. I will more fully address the issue of lies/deception and good intentions as we get into the details of my argument.

Second, trust creates vulnerability. In the act of trusting, we make ourselves vulnerable to breaches of trust. In this way, the trusting relationship itself alters power positions even though we may still have relative equality between individuals. For example, in a mutual love relationship between two adults we hope the two join this relationship as equals and in that sense neither is in a position of power over the other. However, in entering this type of relationship, each now has a kind of power over the other. Each could betray the other's trust and, in this sense, the trust relationship creates an inherent vulnerability. In a situation of trust between people who are not equals, this vulnerability increases—which brings us to our third important aspect of the trust relationship. Given the power invested in the one trusted, the trusted person has a moral responsibility to not exploit the vulnerability of the trusting person. Again, this responsibility is even more important in relationships of inequality.

Given this general account of trust, Potter focuses most of her attention on what it means to be a trustworthy person. In general, a trustworthy person will work to increase trust and decrease mistrust. In keeping with an Aristotelian account of virtue, she argues that: "*A trustworthy person . . . is one who can be counted on, as a matter of the sort of person he or she is, to take care of those things that others entrust to one and* (following the Doctrine of the Mean) *whose ways of caring are neither excessive nor deficient*" (Emphasis in original. Potter 2002, 16). However, to understand what this means in relation to specific actions, we have to take account of the trust relationships in which a particular person is involved. Again, this is especially important in unequal relationships as Potter argues that a trustworthy person will also be non-exploitive and non-dominating.

TRUST IN THE PARENT-CHILD RELATIONSHIP

For my argument, let us assume that the parent-child relationship begins in infancy. In the beginning of the parent-child relationship, trust is relatively simple. The infant "trusts" the parent to tend to her physical needs and from this an emotional attachment quickly develops. I use scare quotes because some would question the use of trust here. Many of the infant's reactions (such as suckling) are instinctual. However, I believe we can call this trust at a very early stage. Research shows that newborns quickly recognize their mother's voice, face, and scent (Gropnik, Meltzoff, and Kuhl 1999; "What Your Baby Knows about You" 2010). Also, infants quickly develop a preference for some caregivers over others. In this way, the infant trusts the primary caregiver(s) to tend to her emotional needs as well as her physical ones.

We see here that the child develops an intimate and trusting relationship with her parent before she is rational. The initial relationship is based on physical needs and recognition of the individual(s) providing them. Since a child has already developed a trusting relationship with her parents, she will continue to trust her parents as she becomes more aware and begins to learn about the world.

As I mentioned earlier, Potter asks us to pay attention to power differences in relationships of trust. To be a trustworthy person, the trusted person must not misuse the power she has over the trusting person.

> The inherent vulnerability in trust, coupled with the vulnerability of the too-readily-trusting person, suggests that those who hold positions of authority or are in institutional roles need to be on guard against inadvertently taking advantage of the readily trusting person. (Potter 2002, 18)

Infants and young children are by nature "too-readily-trusting-persons." The combination of the need to trust and the extreme inequality make young children exceptionally vulnerable. This means parents have an even greater obligation to not exploit that trust. Yet, when parents deceive children about their origins, this is exactly what parents do.

Since a child develops a trusting relationship with her parents before questions about the nature of that relationship surface, the parents have the power to shape how the child comes to understand the parent-child relationship. As the child becomes more aware and begins to develop an understanding of herself and her family, she will trust that her parents are being honest with her about the nature of that relationship. Since parents understand the cultural meaning of these relationships, they also know that the child will assume a biological relationship unless she is told otherwise. This is a form of exploitation in the sense that the parent is using the trust of the child to perpetuate a falsehood. The parent knows the child trusts him and that the child will assume a biological relationship unless she is told otherwise. Therefore, the parent is exploiting (i.e., taking advantage of) the child's trusting nature. Allowing the child to believe a falsehood also constitutes a breach of trust because the child trusts the parent will be a reliable guide in helping the child understand her social world.

Let me clarify that in making this argument I am not trying to privilege genetic parenthood or undermine the importance of social parenting. I do not believe the genetic connection, itself, is the issue. It is the deception that is the problem, and, in committing this particular deception, the parent makes genetics a bigger issue than it needs to be. If the parent is honest with the child from the beginning, then the lack of a genetic relationship simply becomes part of the family narrative. However, if the parent deceives a child about the biological relationship, then this is a breach of trust.

I also believe that it is a greater moral harm to use the trusting relationship itself to help perpetuate a deception. As Sissela Bok argues in her analysis of lying, lying in a relationship of trust is even more grievous because it is usually the trust relationship itself that allows the lie to be efficacious (Bok 1999). Similarly, I believe part of the betrayal in the case of deceiving non-biological children is how the deceiver used the trust relationship to perpetuate the deceit. We have seen that trust in the parent-child relationship is established before the child learns about social categories. Thus, the parent has the power to shape the child's understanding of "Mommy" or "Daddy" (as well as other social categories). The fact that the child does not ask direct questions about her biological origins is a result of her trusting her parents. In this way, it is the intimacy and trust of the parent-child relationship itself that allows the deception to be efficacious.

To summarize my initial argument, children are exceedingly vulnerable in the parent-child relationship. They are forced into an intimate and trusting relationship that is also characterized by extreme inequality. For these reasons, parents have an even greater moral obligation to not violate this trust. Yet, this is exactly what they do when they deceive children about their origins. Children trust their parents and parents are in a unique position to shape their children's understanding of familial relationships. In addition, it is the nature of the relationship itself that allows the deception to be efficacious. Using the trust relationship to perpetuate deceit is also a moral wrong. This is not the sort of behavior in which a trustworthy person would participate. A trustworthy person will be non-exploitive, yet here we have parents exploiting the trust a child has given them to perpetuate a deceit.

At this point, one might object to my initial argument by claiming this is not a significant deception. If we believe genetics is not important in the parent-child relationship, then the parents have not done the child any harm by withholding this information. In fact, if we truly value social parents (which I do), then we could say these parents are fulfilling the necessary and important roles of parenthood and, therefore, are fairly and accurately representing those roles to the child. In other words, we could ask: How do we want a child to understand the category of parent? If our answer rests mainly on social roles and personal relationships, then why must a parent reveal the lack of a genetic connection? To answer this question, I turn now to a more in-depth analysis of trust within intimate relationships.

A FOUNDATIONAL LIE

Part of my argument is that deceiving a child about her origins is a moral wrong because it is a lie about the nature of the relationship itself. For this reason, I call it a "foundational" lie. Some have questioned the use of lie here instead of continuing to call it a deception. I believe some forms of deception amount to a kind of lie. After all we do recognize lies of omission. In this case a parent is allowing (encouraging?) a child to adopt a certain understanding of social categories and relationships while knowing that understanding is false. It seems a kind of excuse or rationalization to say this is not a lie just because the person never explicitly utters the words "I am your biological parent." For this reason, I will begin to use lies and deception interchangeably when discussing our primary example. Also, as we get into this section, we will see that in order to maintain the deception, parents are likely to have to use more overt lies—especially in relation to family and medical history.

To explain why this type of lie is foundational, I turn now to Potter's analysis of intimacy and trust. Potter argues that the main feature of intimacy is a kind of connection that is not possible without trust.

> I will argue that intimacy requires a quality of relation captured by the concept of *connection* and that being connected in intimate relations requires that we be trustworthy. Being in an intimate relationship, therefore, involves an ongoing effort to be trustworthy and to sustain trust with one another. (Emphasis in original. Potter 2002, 121)

I previously argued that trust in the parent-child relationship is initially based on physical and emotional closeness. We now see how this relates to Potter's understanding of connection and intimacy. For Potter, connection is established mainly through a variety of shared experiences. In infancy and early childhood, the shared experiences will primarily be physical and emotional. There are few relationships more physically intimate than the one between a caregiver and a small child. The parent must tend to all of the child's physical needs. The child will also come to depend on the parent for emotional comfort. In this way, an intimate trust relationship is established even before the child can talk. However, trust is a dynamic concept and so we must be attuned to what it means to *remain* trustworthy as the relationship changes.

In infancy and very early childhood, the idea of biological origins is clearly not an issue. However, once the child becomes a toddler, she will begin to take an interest in names, categories, and relationships. Mommies, Daddies, Aunts, and Grandmas are all part of our family. Teachers, friends, and people we meet on the elevator have a different status. As a child moves through the preschool age and into early childhood, she develops a more sophisticated notion of these categories—especially how they are defined in the culture. If a child is being raised by a gay couple, she will begin to notice her family makeup is perhaps different from that of some of her friends. Assuming the child is in a supportive environment, this is not a bad thing or a cause for concern. I simply use this example to illustrate how children become aware of these category distinctions and begin to develop an understanding of their family story and how it relates to the cultural understandings of these categories.[3]

As the child continues to grow her understanding of these categories becomes more sophisticated. As Potter explains, if we want to maintain trust, then we need to be attuned to what it means to remain trustworthy as the relationship grows and changes. My point here is that parents are given a relationship of trust that developed in infancy. Yet, as the child grows, she trusts the parents to do more and different things. Here we are discussing the child's trust in a parent to be a reliable navigator in learning about social relationships. If the parent perpetuates this deception, then he is not being a reliable navigator and, thus, violates that trust.

So far we have been focused on the "ongoing effort to be trustworthy," but shared experiences are also a significant part of Potter's understanding of the connection necessary for intimacy. As Potter explains, we need connection for intimacy and shared experiences create connection, but sometimes a fear of difference undermines the very connection we are trying to make.

> A longing for connection may motivate us to act in ways that hamper the very thing we want. And we may want connection so badly that we lose sight of what it means for us to be trustworthy to this person in this moment. This sort of thing can happen when we are confronted with differences that we believe will threaten a connection. (Potter 2002, 130)

If we are worried that our differences will undermine the relationship, we have a tendency to tell small lies to cover up these differences. Potter argues we should avoid these forms of dishonesty because they actually undermine the very connection we are trying to make.

Which brings us to another feature of trustworthiness that facilitates the connection necessary for intimacy—honesty. Potter argues that we need not disclose everything to be trustworthy in an intimate relationship. We must be attuned to the nature and context of the relationship to decide what needs to be disclosed and what can be withheld. In thinking about my example, there are many things that parents may choose to keep from their children (say details about their sex life or embarrassing aspects of their past). Yet, to be trustworthy and to foster connection, we must also be honest. If our nondisclosure helps to perpetuate a deception, then we are not being honest, and failing to be honest makes us untrustworthy. Yet, clearly, there are certain deceptions that we seem to readily tolerate in intimate relationships and do not see these as a violation of our requirement to be honest. For example, if I am planning a surprise party for my husband, he will probably not be bothered by the lies I tell in the short term to pull off the party. In situations like this, we seem to have a sort of agreement that this is not a "real" deception or form of dishonesty. Thus, we need to think a bit more about disclosure, honesty, and deception.

In general, intimacy requires connection, connection requires honesty, and honesty requires avoiding deception. However, we have seen that intimacy and trust do not require total disclosure about all things. Sometimes we can hold back parts of ourselves and sometimes deceptions are tolerated. To sort out when honesty and disclosure are necessary and what kinds of deceptions undermine trustworthiness, I have introduced the idea of a foundational lie.

If a significant part of connection is shared experiences, then I cannot build connection by lying about that shared experience. If the person finds out I am lying about these shared interests upon which our relationship is built, then it not only undermines the person's trust in me, but also her trust in the relationship itself. This is because when the person thought we were experiencing a connection, I was lying about that connection. For this reason, I call these sorts of lies foundational lies. By calling into question the connections we have, they undermine the very foundation of the relationship.

For example, Potter says we are often tempted to tell lies when we have differences that we are afraid will hamper connection. We want connection to build intimacy which is necessary for relationships, but connection requires trust. Consider the following example. I am beginning to build a relationship with someone who has the potential to be a good friend. In an attempt to foster connection, I pretend to like her favorite band. Suppose the relationship grows and we have now been friends for three years. In that time we have shared many experiences and have discovered many mutual interests beyond music. We have a lot in common and get along very well. However, in the beginning of our relationship, I lied about liking the same music because I knew this was her favorite band and I was afraid this difference would make her not like me or want to hang out. Due to this lie, we have had numerous conversations about this band, attended concerts together, and she has given me gifts of this band's music. Now, three years later, she finds out I do not like this band. Despite the fact that we are quite compatible and have many other mutual interests, this lie will threaten our friendship because it is what I call a foundational lie. It is a lie about some of the shared experiences and connections upon which our relationship was founded. As such, it will lead her to question those experiences and connections.

If we return to the issue of lying to children about their biological origins, it should now be clear why this is a foundational lie. It is often the parents' fear of difference that motivates the lie. However, in perpetuating this lie, parents undermine the very connection they are trying to make. For the deception to be successful, the parents will have to pretend to share connections with the child that do not exist. Here I think the undermining of shared connections is more subtle than in the music example, but it is no less damaging. Think of the importance of family history to personal identity for many people. We are connected to our ethnic heritage, our religious background, our medical history, and our personal family story. In a family that lies about a child's biological origins, these seemingly benign family stories will be tainted. Perhaps this child feels connected to her Irish ancestors and the discrimination they experienced as new immigrants when her past is actually traced to Germans who arrived much later.

Again, my point is not to argue for the primacy of genetic connections. I believe it ultimately makes no difference if the child's heritage is Irish or German. I also acknowledge that children and parents can and do have many other shared experiences that foster connection. I can assume the parent honestly loves the child and does all the normal things parents would do to help their child grow and flourish (see previous chapters). Despite all of this, I am trying to show how this particular deception is detrimental to the relationship in the way my perpetuating a significant lie for many years would (if discovered) undermine my friendship. I would also argue that, even if the deception is not discovered, it can potentially threaten the relationship by tainting other experiences. For example, lying about a child's genetic origins leads to any number of deceits that ultimately threaten to undermine the social connection that we are trying to foster. If parents were honest about the child's genetic heritage, she may still feel solidarity with the history of her non-blood relatives. However, she would not feel betrayed by the innumerable lies that were necessary to perpetuate the deception about her origins. Similarly, I doubt my friend would have really cared that much if I admitted I did not like her favorite band. However, she would rightly care a lot about the fact that I perpetuated this lie for three years.

These types of lies also undermine the connection necessary for intimacy because one person has to hide a significant part of who he or she really is. Or, perhaps in this case it is more accurate to say that a person has to continually misrepresent himself or herself. While it is true that we do not have to disclose everything about ourselves to foster intimacy, I believe this becomes a kind of misrepresentation that undermines the connection necessary for intimacy. For example, families often casually reference things like "cancer runs on your mom's side of the family" or "it is common for people on your dad's side of the family to have twins." When the child is a product of "donor" gametes we may not know if this is true or we may know it is definitely not true. Regardless, these proclamations will have a different feel to them. They will not be viewed by the parent as casual or innocent remarks because the parent is aware of the deception lurking behind them. In fact, there is evidence that children sense this tension in the family even when they are not aware of the deception (McGee, Brakman, and Gurmankin 2001). Thus, lying about being a child's genetic parent becomes a tainted thread that runs through the course of the relationship. Much like we cannot help but notice an off-color thread woven into a tapestry, this lie will constantly be present as the parent works to maintain the deception. This not only threatens the connection necessary for intimacy, but also undermines the parent's trustworthiness.

In this way, I believe lying to children about their genetic heritage is a breach of trust that shakes the foundation of the parent-child relationship. It is a deception about the nature of the relationship and, ultimately, about some of the shared experiences that are the foundation of the relationship. It also requires an ongoing deception about the participants in the relationship. The parent must misrepresent part of who he or she is as well as hiding part of the child's past from himself or herself. In these ways, the original deception runs through the relationship like a tainted thread spun into a tapestry. Therefore, even though parents and children share many other experiences, this type of deception undermines the very intimacy the parents are trying to foster.

A PRACTICAL OBJECTION

I have argued that lying to children about their biological origins is a breach of trust in the parent-child relationship that continues to erode a parent's trustworthiness. Therefore, a trustworthy parent would not participate in this deception. I can imagine some might agree with much of my analysis but then claim there are other reasons this lie might be morally justified. In other words, one might argue that there are good reasons for perpetuating this lie that override the potential moral wrong I have identified. In closing, I will deal with this potential objection by considering various reasons parents give for withholding this information.

In "Gamete Donation and Anonymity," Glenn McGee and his colleagues summarize the reasons given for lying to children about their genetic origins:

> to ensure that the non-genetic parent be perceived as equally connected to the child, to ensure that the child grows as strong a bond with that parent as with the genetic parent, to maintain the appearance of a "normal" family, to avoid distressing the child with the truth of his/her origin, and to allow the non-genetic parent's infertility—a condition that usually carries a negative stigma

with it—to remain unknown to others. (McGee, Brakman, and Gurmankin 2001, 2034)

Here we see a combination of self-motivated and altruistic reasons. Reasons such as trying to appear "normal" and hiding one partner's infertility are clearly self-motivated. If being trustworthy is part of being a virtuous parent, then I do not believe these reasons can be justified. But what about reasons such as trying to ensure that the child bonds with the non-genetic parent or trying to avoid distressing the child? Could these more altruistic reasons be used to justify the deception? I do not believe these reasons can be justified either.

In her discussion of lying to children, Sissela Bok points out that some people believe it is okay to lie to children simply because they are children. She dismisses this argument out of hand, but admits that it is often *easier* to lie to children. Since children do not have the same powers of judgment or reason, we often bend the truth in certain ways to guide children's behavior for the best or to protect them from dangers. In this way, it is very easy to slip into any number of paternalistic lies when dealing with children. In the case we are considering, lying to a child about her biological origins to avoid distressing a child could be a paternalistic lie. The question we need to ask is if it can be justified based on altruistic motives.

Given the ease of lying to children, Bok argues that we should require extra justification for lying to children. "Rather than accepting the common view, therefore, that it is somehow more justifiable to lie to children and to those the liars regard as being *like* children, special precautions are needed in order to not exploit them" (Emphasis in original. Bok 1999, 218). She does not specify exactly what these precautions should be; however, in much of her discussion, she asks us to use the perspective of the deceived to judge whether lying is justified. Lies to children are often justified on paternalistic grounds, but Bok believes, if we take the perspective of the deceived, we will find that the "altruistic" motives often hide self-protective motives and manipulation (Bok 1999, 212).

Instead of saving children from distress, research shows that lying often causes more distress. In fact, most research shows honesty usually leads to very positive outcomes for the entire family. When children are told early and in a developmentally appropriate way, the disclosure simply becomes part of the family narrative (McGee, Brakman, and Gurmankin 2001, 2034). In contrast, children who found out later in life or via third parties about their origins were "resentful and suspect, and the betrayal of trust caused irreparable damage to family relationships" (McGee, Brakman, and Gurmankin 2001, 2034).[4] If these studies are correct, then most children are not distressed by knowing the truth about their origins. What children are distressed by is the breach of trust in the parent-child relationship.[5] Thus, I would argue that these "altruistic" reasons are often more likely rationalizations.

So far I have argued that most reasons given for lying to children are unjustified even if they initially appear to have altruistic motives. In the last part of this section, I want to devote some space to one of the most common reasons for lying to children—fear of rejection. Many parents who use "donor" gametes fear that the children will not consider them to be "real" parents. For example, here is Richard discussing his fears:

> We did not know anyone who had adult DI [Donor Insemination] children and my greatest fear was that I would be rejected by my children in favour of, as I saw it, their "real" father. I said to Heather many times, "You will always be their mother." I felt I was jeopardizing my relationship, but my wife had nothing to lose. (Lorbach 2003, 115)

Here we are reminded of how the vulnerability in a trusting relationship goes both ways. I have argued that children are exceptionally vulnerable due to the extreme inequality and the power parents have to shape the nature of the relationship. Yet, we must also recognize that parents are vulnerable as well. In entering this intimate and loving relationship with a child, parents also are vulnerable to disappointment and rejection.

While it is important to acknowledge the fear and vulnerability of the parents, our earlier analysis shows that a trustworthy person should resist the temptation to lie. Potter acknowledges that people are often tempted to lie out of a fear of difference—specifically if they fear differences will undermine the connection necessary for intimacy. In contrast, Potter argues it is the lie (not the differences) that undermine the connection because the lie erodes the trust necessary for connection.

To see why, let me briefly return to our discussion of trust in intimacy. We discussed how intimacy requires connection and connection requires trust. To maintain the trust necessary for connection we must also have relational awareness which requires a deep level of honesty.

> We have to be able and willing to be honest with ourselves, for example, in assessing how we are feeling about the relationship, and we have to be able to be honest with ourselves and others at particular moments within that relationship. But being honest in this deep way—about how one is feeling, about what one needs and wants from the other, about what is satisfying in a relationship and what isn't—is very difficult when we don't trust the other person. (Potter 2002, 136)

Deep honesty is both difficult and dynamic. I must be honest about my own needs, feelings, and motives. We have seen that when parents in this situation are honest with themselves about their own feelings and motives, we find that often the primary reason to lie to children is a fear of rejection. Yet, both our theory and the empirical evidence argue against perpetuating this deception.

As we saw in the first section, infants and young children innately trust their caregiver(s) so initial bonding is not an issue. If we look at how children fair in families that disclose the child's non-genetic origins, we see that most children have no difficulty in maintaining their bond with the non-genetic parent(s)—especially if they are told when they are young.

> The next day they [the children] made up a little card on the computer, with, "Thank you, we love you both," all that sort of stuff. It was so touching, it was so thoughtful. When I told them I said that it was best to be honest with them and I think they appreciate that. I think they've grown up to really appreciate what that meant for us, how hard it was. (Lorbach 2003, 123)

Here we see that even though the fear of rejection is a primary reason for lying to children, the children seem very accepting and adaptable when parents are honest with them. Also, instead of threatening family bonds, many parents feel relief about the disclosure and view their honesty as a way to improve trust in the parent-child relationship (Mendell and Benward 2009). For example, here is Richard after telling his children: "What a weight I feel lifted off me now there are no more secrets. We can build on trust now that all the cards are on the table" (Lorbach 2003, 134). Many parents mention the issue of trust in deciding to be honest with their children. I would argue that they understand how this lie erodes their trustworthiness and, conversely, how being honest reinforces their trustworthy character.

To summarize, I have shown why it is immoral to lie to children about their origins. It is a breach of trust in the parent-child relationship that harms the liar as well as the deceived. While I do not have space to argue for it here, I believe this moral argument has practical implications. Perhaps we should make it harder (instead of easier) for parents to perpetuate this deception. For example, we could revise birth certificates to include all people who participated in bringing this child into the world. Also, it makes little sense to say children should be told of their origins, but not allow children any further information about their genetic parents. A logical consequence would be to end the practice of anonymous gamete "donation." However, these arguments go beyond the scope of this paper. Here I focus on the need for trust and honesty within the parent-child relationship.

CODA: SOME THOUGHTS ON SANTA CLAUS

When I originally wrote this chapter, I received questions about how I would address the issue of Santa Claus or the Easter Bunny. At the time, this was beyond the scope of what I wanted to address in this book, but now I would like to add a few thoughts on this kind of issue. In short, I would say that we should not lie to children about these imaginary figures; however, if parents do, I do not believe the long-term implications are comparable to lying about a child's genetic origins. Let me explain.

Given the theory I have proposed here, I believe it is generally wrong to try and convince children that Santa Claus is real. This is not only a deception (coming from someone they trust), but it is often a very elaborate deception. There is a whole history surrounding this character and children are often encouraged to write letters to him or visit him at the mall. More recently, parents are adding supporting characters such as the "Elf on the Shelf" who reports back to Santa. In this way, parents create a whole world the child is invited into, only to later discover it is all an elaborate hoax. Incidentally, this is also why I believe many people remember when they learned that Santa Claus was not real. It shifted their understanding of the world and their parents.

Another reason I would argue against this kind of deception is that I do not believe it is necessary.[6] At the time parents are usually introducing their children to Santa Claus (and the stories and rituals), children are very open to imaginative play. Thus, it seems reasonable that children would enjoy the rituals and experience just as much even if it were presented as a game (or in some other format that did not require Santa to be "real"). Indeed, this is a time when children are still sometimes confusing reality and fantasy so they may more or less treat Santa as "real" even without the parents working to perpetuate this idea. Either way, my guess is that children would still enjoy the holiday and associated rituals even if they know Santa is a fictional character.

For all of these reasons, I would say it is best to not lie to your children about Santa Claus; however, I will concede that I do not believe this kind of deception has the same kind of long-term implications that something like lying about genetic origins does. While many people remember when they learned that Santa Claus was not real, most people do not harbor any long-term resentment about this issue. Some are initially very angry or upset, but they also recognize the good-natured intentions behind the rituals and, thus, are ultimately okay with it. However, I would like to point out that part of this also has to do with the ubiquitous nature of Christmas and Santa Claus in the United States. I can imagine if a parent picked some random character to convince their child was real and create various elaborate rituals around this character, then children might feel this to be a more malicious kind of deception.

In sum, I believe a virtuous parent should be a kind of role model. If we want children to learn to trust those with whom they have intimate and loving relationships, then we should practice behaviors that foster that trust. This would almost always tilt the scales toward honesty. To be clear, as any parent knows, there will likely be some occasions in which a small lie is justified to keep the peace or get things done. In contrast, large scale deceptions and lying about how the world works are likely to erode trust. As parents, we are mentors and role models—we should act accordingly.

NOTES

1. The original version of this chapter was published in *Philosophy and the Contemporary World* (Vol. 18/No. 2: Fall 2011).

2. Since people seldom give away their gametes for free, I use scare quotes around "donor." Sperm and egg vendors would be a more accurate term.

3. In *Reinventing the Family*, Laurie Benkov has an extended discussion of how gay and lesbian families try to sort out what language to use as parents and how to present these relationships to others (Benkov 1994).

4. It should be noted that the study being discussed here was on adopted children who found out later in life. However, we can imagine there would be similar results for children conceived using third-party gametes.

5. Many children are also upset that they cannot find out identifying information about their genetic parents (Daniels 2007; Lorbach 2003), but that issue goes beyond the scope of the argument I am making here.

6. Indeed, there are many children (e.g., Jewish kids) who grow up perfectly happy without ever participating in the ritual of Santa Claus or Christmas.

Chapter Five

Shaping Bodies, Shaping Lives

Parental Authority and the Child's Future

In this chapter, I consider the scope of parental decision making focusing mainly on decisions that limit or foreclose future options for the child. My discussion will include two cases that involve permanent body modifications—intersex surgeries and cochlear implants, and one case that does not involve permanently foreclosing future options—transgender children. Most theorists currently approach these issues using a rights-based framework. Using these cases, I will show why a virtue theory approach can focus our attention on other morally salient features that can help construct a more nuanced analysis. Specifically, a virtue theory approach shifts our attention from an attempt to maximize autonomy and choice to, instead, consider the nature of the parent-child relationship and the context in which these decisions are made.

THE CASES

Here I briefly introduce three general cases or issues for us to consider as we assess the scope and nature of parental decision making.

Case #1: Intersex Infants

There are a variety of medical disorders that can cause children to have ambiguous genitalia.[1] In the 1950s, the medical community created a new protocol for dealing with these cases. Influenced by Freud's theories of sexual development, John Money argued that, until around eighteen to twenty-four months of age, children's gender identification was fluid. Therefore, if we choose a gender for a child shortly after birth and unwaveringly committed to raising the child in this gender, then everything would be fine. In order for everyone to be committed to the chosen gender, it was deemed necessary to surgically alter any ambiguity in the genitalia. Also, the children could never be told about what had happened. The parents must maintain the illusion that there was no ambiguity related to the child's gender or biological sex. This was problematic for a number of reasons including the fact that many of these surgeries required various follow-up treatments and, later, hormone regimens.

In the late 1980s and into the 1990s, as many of these children were now well into their adult years, they began to find out what had happened to them. Many felt betrayed by both their parents and the medical community. In addition, many had ongoing physical issues. Some had medical issues with pain or problems with urination. Others had been made infertile or lost sexual sensation due to the nature of the surgeries performed. In 1993, Cheryl Chase founded the Intersex Society of North America [ISNA]. Through this group, Chase and other activists began to argue against performing medically unnecessary surgeries on infants who could not consent.

After many years of activism, the tide has turned. Most now agree that we should avoid medically unnecessary surgeries on infants ("Intersex Society of North America / A World Free of Shame, Secrecy, and Unwanted Genital Surgery" n.d.). The current recommendations are to raise the child as whichever gender we would expect the child to identify with when he or she is older, but to not perform any cosmetic surgery that would foreclose other options. When the children are older, they will be allowed to decide if they prefer the chosen gender or would like to transition to another gender. However, these surgeries have not been outlawed and do still continue to happen. As the ISNA website points out, consensus statements and policy recommendations are slow to take effect in the larger medical community. Therefore, this is still a decision presented to parents.

Case #2: Cochlear Implants

For children born with significant hearing loss, cochlear implants offer the hope of oral language and an easier time navigating the hearing world.[2] This technology allows children with significant hearing loss to hear, but it does not perfectly mimic what a "normal" person would hear. Also, there is some uncertainty about how well it will work for any specific child. However, it generally works well enough to allow those with significant hearing loss to learn oral speech and function much like a non-hearing impaired person would.[3] In order to achieve this level of success, the implants need to be introduced while the children are still infants or toddlers. It is especially important that children learn to identify various sounds as early as possible—

this helps train the brain for oral speech and language. As such, the decision to use cochlear implants is usually made well before the child is able to be part of this conversation.

The decision to use cochlear implants will shape the child's future—opening some options but foreclosing others. First, the implants will destroy any residual hearing. So while it is possible to turn them off later in life, it will rule out the option of using more traditional hearing aids. Also, while it is possible to teach oral communication and American Sign Language (ASL) at the same time, the use of cochlear implants will affect brain development. Training for sound will create different pathways than training in ASL alone. Finally, early use of cochlear implants can significantly influence the development of oral speech and that will affect the child's ability to function in the hearing world.

Needless to say, the introduction of this technology created a firestorm in the deaf community. Many who are deaf see themselves as a minority culture. In addition to certain lifestyle modifications, ASL is a unique language with its own structure and grammar. For these reasons, many saw cochlear implants as an attack on their culture and way of life. The deaf community has softened their stance a bit on cochlear implants, but they are still very wary of them and encourage medical professionals to put hearing parents who have deaf children in touch with those in the deaf community. As the National Association for the Deaf correctly states, medical professionals are experts on the inner ear, but "they should not be viewed as, nor should they function as, experts with regard to larger issues such as the educational, psychological, social, and linguistic needs of the deaf child" ("Position Statement on Cochlear Implants" 2015).

Case #3: Transgender Children

In this last case, we are not immediately confronted with permanent body modifications. For transgender youth, medical decisions will not come until puberty. Even then, the decision to use puberty-blocking hormones is reversible—merely buying time until the children are old enough to consent to permanent surgical transition. Still the decision to allow or not allow a transgender child to live as his or her chosen gender can have significant implications for the child's development. For example, in *Becoming Nicole*, Wyatt Maines declared at an early age that "he" was a girl (or a girl-boy as she initially called herself). Nicole (her chosen name) enjoyed traditionally feminine games, toys, and clothing styles. As she got older and began school, the desire to live as a girl only increased. Thus, her parents were confronted with significant decisions such as whether to allow or encourage Nicole's gender expression and, later, whether to intervene on her behalf with the school (Nutt 2016).

Even though these decisions do not include permanent body modifications or other actions that would permanently foreclose future options for Nicole, they are still life-altering decisions. I will show how the case of a young child wanting to express her lived gender challenges the rights-based approach. It also helps explain why it is more important to focus on the lived parent-child experience.

WHAT'S WRONG WITH RIGHTS?

Many debates over parental decisions related to prenatal choices or body modifications focus on autonomy and rights—specifically parental autonomy versus a child's future autonomy. This is often framed as a question about how we balance a parent's right to make decisions for her child against the child's future autonomy or ability to make his own choices. Drawing on the work of Joel Feinberg, this entire debate has come to be known as a debate over the child's right to an open future.

In "The Child's Right to an Open Future," Feinberg begins by articulating different kinds of rights. There are A-C rights that are common to adults and children. These are basic rights to be free from violation or harm. Then there are A rights that belong only to adults. These are the rights you would expect any competent adult to have such as the ability to vote or decisions about freedom of movement. Finally, there are C rights, which apply mainly to children but may sometimes apply to adults. Here we have two subgroups: dependency rights (which apply to things like food or shelter) and "rights-in-trust" (which will be the focus of our discussion). Given that, in the normal course of development, children will eventually become autonomous adults, Feinberg argues that children have "rights-in-trust," which include most of the autonomy rights we grant adults. The idea is that the nurturing adult must hold these rights (try not to foreclose them) until the child is able to exercise them. Feinberg summarizes this using the phrase "right to an open future."

In his analysis of the parent-child relationship, Feinberg admits that, at some stages, paternalism is perfectly justifiable. Children are not autonomous adults and, thus, sometimes a caring parent needs to protect them from their lack of judgment. Also, it is impossible for children to remain a blank slate until they reach adulthood. Parents can and should instill their children with some set of values. Yet, this seems to create a paradox:

> In a nutshell: the parents help create some of the interests whose fulfillment will constitute the child's own good. They cannot aim at an independent conception of the child's own good in deciding how to do this, because to some extent, the child's own good (self-fulfillment) depends on which interests the parents decide to create. (Feinberg 1992, 95)

In other words, the decisions a child makes when he is an adult will often be based on a character or self largely shaped by parental influences.

Feinberg resolves this paradox by pointing out how growth is a collective endeavor between the child and parent. Even at birth the child has certain dispositions and talents. A parent should help discover these talents and dispositions and then encourage the child to develop them.

> Thus from the beginning the child must—inevitably *will*—have some "input" in its own shaping, the extent of which will grow continuously even as the child's character itself does. I think that we can avoid, or at least weaken, the paradoxes if we remember that the child can contribute toward the making of his own self and circumstances in ever-increasing degrees. (Emphasis in original. Feinberg 1992, 96)

In sum, Feinberg believes we can avoid this paradox by acknowledging the role children play in their own development, encouraging parents to respect the child's ever-increasing autonomy and to nurture the child's obvious talents and dispositions, and leaving open as many future options as possible.

While this sounds good in the abstract, Feinberg leaves much ambiguity in the details. For example, Feinberg discusses court cases where the adults' right to freedom of religion potentially clashes with the child's right to an open future. In *Wisconsin v. Yoder*, the state sued the Amish community for violating a state law that required children to attend school through age sixteen. The Supreme Court found in favor of the Amish community and declared this a violation of freedom of religion. Ultimately, Feinberg agrees claiming that an extra two years of education cannot make that large of a difference in shaping the children's future. Also, he claims that to decide otherwise would threaten the Amish way of life—which Feinberg sees as an undue imposition on parental rights. Yet, this is a surprising conclusion given that he agrees the lack of education makes it difficult for children to leave the Amish community. I am left wondering how this is not a violation of the child's right to an open future.

Indeed, Dena Davis, using Feinberg's right to an open future argument, argues against the parents in this case. When the courts decided in favor of the Amish parents, Davis claims:

> No justice squarely faced the question of whether the liberal democratic state owes all its citizens, especially children, a right to a basic education that can serve as a building block if the child decides later in life that she wishes to become an astronaut, a playwrite, or perhaps to join the army. (Davis 1997a, 10)

She goes on to reiterate that it is commonly held that lack of a high school diploma greatly restricts one's future options—questioning whether this is a decision parents should be allowed to make for their children.

Part of the disagreement between Davis and Feinberg rests on how big of a difference those extra two years of schooling would make. In the court case, the Amish argue that it makes a huge difference. Not only do they believe that the kind of things students would learn go against the basic education promoted by their religion, but they also argue that their religion requires children at this age to begin a different kind of education. This is when children begin a sort of apprenticeship to adult relatives that teaches them the kinds of skills they will need to have to fulfill their roles in the community. The Amish claim it also inculcates in children the values of the community such as an appreciation for hard work. Davis and Feinberg both seem to agree that this court case tilts the scales in favor of parental autonomy. Davis points out how the extra education would not only allow children greater future job opportunities, but she also agrees with the Amish community that this education might make it difficult for the children to be satisfied or happy living the simple Amish lifestyle. In this way, insisting on greater education may foreclose the option of choosing to remain within the Amish community because the child's attitudes and desires have been led in a different direction. As Davis points out, this means that it is impossible for the state to remain neutral here—either decision will tilt the scales one way or another.

Feinberg argues that requiring the extra two years of education does not make a large difference in future opportunities and, thus, would be too great of an imposition on parental autonomy. Even though he admits that this makes it difficult for the children to choose an alternative lifestyle, he seems to think the scales are already weighted in that direction and so it is best to side with the parents. If, later in life the child wants to leave based on her own "values, talents, and propensities" it would be difficult, but not impossible for her to do so. As we see, Davis makes the opposite call. Her argument uses Feinberg's idea of maximizing future options, but she also draws on the part of Feinberg's theory that says parents should be alert to a child's talents and propensities and work to cultivate them. Davis states, "The problem with this is that, as I understand the Amish way of life, being Amish is precisely not to make one's life choices on the basis of one's own 'talents and propensities,' but to subordinate those individual leanings to the traditions of the group" (Davis 1997a, 11). For Davis, it is okay for to have anti-liberal groups within a liberal, democratic state *as long as individuals are free to join or leave as they choose.* She believes the Yoder decision undermines the Amish children's ability to choose to leave.

This disagreement between Davis and Feinberg in relation to the Yoder case illustrates the weakness in Feinberg's theory. It would seem that a child's right to choose their own religious affiliation as an adult would clearly be a right-in-trust as Feinberg defines them. Indeed, I think Feinberg does see this as a protected right. Yet, when faced with the Yoder case, he chooses in favor of parental autonomy. As Davis points out, not only does this seem to violate his basic understanding of rights-in-trust, it also ignores his claim that parents should cultivate a child's natural propensities and talents. Feinberg adds this caveat as a way to show how children play a role in the creation of their own future desires or understanding of the good, but he seems willing to sacrifice this aspect of his theory in order to respect the parent's right to religious freedom. We also see from this dispute that our debate over where this case should fall in Feinberg's theory takes us beyond Feinberg's theory. Ultimately, Davis considers this case in relation to the values and policies of a liberal democratic state.

To emphasize the problem here, I turn to Joseph Millum's critique of Feinberg's right to an open future. Millum claims that the right to an open future, as Feinberg argues for it, is underdetermined. Specifically, Feinberg explains that the "rights-in-trust" held by children are coextensive with the autonomy rights of adults. This would seem to argue for a "maximally open future." However, Millum claims that the kind of arguments Feinberg gives do not support this strong right. Indeed, we have seen that Feinberg, himself, does not seem to support a "maximally open future." Given this, Millum argues that a more moderate argument—"according to which children have a right to acquire some reasonable range of skills and options"—is more plausible. Unfortunately, Feinberg does not give us a way to define what would or would not fall under this more moderate right. As Millum explains:

> Talk of an open future then ends up being unhelpful: it is likely to obscure the detailed arguments that must be provided to defend keeping a child's future open in some particular respect or providing her with particular skills and opportunities. (Millum 2014, 535)

Millum argues that Feinberg gives us no real guidance on how to draw the boundaries of this right and, thus, his argument is normatively empty. I agree with Millum and will take up the kind of discussion he alludes to in the next section. However, before moving on, let us briefly consider how the right to an open future might address our cases under consideration.

Given the variety of harms associated with nonmedical surgeries performed on intersex infants, the right to an open future theory could easily argue against them. For example, many of these surgeries leave the children infertile. The right to reproduce would seem to count as a right-in-trust that should be protected. Davis explicitly claims this as protected right and argues that sterilization violates a child's right to an open future. I believe Feinberg would agree with this as well. He gives an example of a right to walk down the street as a future right a not-yet-walking child will have. He further states that amputating her legs would be a violation of this right. If walking is a protected right, then surely fertility would be as well. Assuming the cosmetic surgery does not sterilize the child, would the open future argument still rule it out? My guess is that it could. In theory, the gender modifications performed are reversible (Kipnis and Diamond 1999); but many of the surgeries leave children with pain and the need for ongoing medical treatments. In this way, they may likely violate the A-C rights to be protected from bodily harm.

While I do believe that the right to an open future theory would protect children from unnecessary surgeries, there is an aspect of this case that I do not believe is adequately addressed by this theory. A significant harm articulated by adults that have had these surgeries is psychological—namely, the betrayal associated with keeping their history a secret. A secret so shameful it cannot be discussed. It is true that adults have a right to medical information, so a right to an open future would argue against this kind of medical secret keeping, but I do not see how a right to an open future addresses the breach in trust in the parent-child relationship. This goes beyond a right to medical information and, instead, speaks to the nature of the relationship itself. Many intersex adults are upset not just because it was a secret, but the nature of the secret made them feel as if their parents were ashamed of them. I do not see how the right to an open future theory can address these kinds of harms. Do children have a right to parental openness? Or parental approval and acceptance?

The decision for or against using cochlear implants is more complicated because there are so many unknowns. As the technology progresses, it does seem that the implants are more and more likely to be successful. If we can assume that using the implant will likely make it possible for children to develop oral speech and be able to function in a hearing world, then I believe the right to an open future theory would have to argue in favor of using it. While she does not explicitly argue in favor of this, Davis seems to imply she would. She discusses the early debate over cochlear implants and poses the question of whether they would be required if success was relatively certain (Davis 1997b). She also strongly argues against allowing deaf parents to use assisted reproductive technology to purposely have a deaf child. Much of her argument here rests on how the parents would be unduly limiting the child's future options. Although, she adds Kantian reasoning to argue that parents should not use children as a means to their own ends. In general, Davis seems to be more willing to override parental autonomy in favor of the child's autonomy than Feinberg does (Davis 1997a). I am unsure what Feinberg would say about this debate. Since children have the option to turn off the implants later in life, my guess is he would generally support their use. Theoretically, using the implant leaves both options open to the future child—existing within the hearing world or submersing himself in deaf culture.

The case of transgender children poses even more difficult questions as it generally does not require any permanent body modifications until the children are old enough (or almost old enough) to exercise their adult autonomy rights. In this way, we are not technically foreclosing any options by requiring the children to live one way or another until they reach maturity. In fact, we have transgender biographies that give accounts of children who were forced to live as their assigned gender and did not transition until adulthood. For older children, we could argue about whether they have a right to puberty-blocking hormones as these will make a significant difference in their ability to successfully transition. In this case, I think Feinberg and Davis would both support a child's right to puberty-blocking hormones. The entire point of using these hormones is to leave future options open. If the child chooses to not transition and wishes to live as his assigned biological gender, the hormones can be discontinued allowing puberty to proceed. Also, Feinberg argues that many adult rights will become active in varying degrees by the time a child is a tween: "Many or most of a child's C rights-in-trust have already become A rights by the time he is ten or twelve. Any 'mere child' beyond the stage of infancy is only a child in some respects, and already an adult in others" (Feinberg 1992, 95). For these reasons, as well as the promotion of the child's propensities and talents kind of arguments, I think Davis and Feinberg would both support allowing transgender children to express their chosen gender even from an early age.

However, it is not clear to me that a child's right to an open future argument can make a robust defense of this position for young children. Feinberg argues that it is a parent's job to socialize children and, in this socialization, it is okay for parents to attempt to instill children with their own values. Given that young children do not have autonomy skills or rights combined with the fact that requiring a child to uphold traditional gender norms does not foreclose the possibility of transitioning later, it is unclear to me how theorists can make a strong argument in favor of allowing young children to express their chosen gender using the child's right to an open future. I think this is especially true if allowing the child to express a different gender violates the parents' religious view. We have seen that Feinberg in particular is wary of unduly burdening a parent's right to raise children in their chosen religion. As we will see in the next section, I think a virtue theory approach gives us a better way to make a case in favor of supporting even young children's ability to live their chosen gender.

As we turn our attention to a virtue theory approach, one key difference is how it highlights other aspects of these cases. Virtue theory naturally shifts our focus from an exercise in trying to map out the proper scope of rights to an analysis of intentions, motivations, and character traits that shape the nature of the relationship. As Millum shows, we need a way to assess which choices should be protected in specific cases. Given the maximizing nature of Feinberg's and Davis's theories, Millum argues we need some other tools for assessing specific decisions—especially if we want to defend a more moderate theory. I believe virtue theory can partially answer Millum's challenge. If we turn our attention to what the child needs to flourish—now and in the future—we are better able to see when and how it may be ethical to foreclose certain options. This is not to say that autonomy is unimportant. Indeed, we discussed in earlier chapters the need to develop moral reasoning (one component of being an autonomous adult). However, given that virtue theory asks different questions, it will shift our attention to other morally salient features of these cases.

A VIRTUE THEORY APPROACH TO PARENTAL DECISIONS

To show how virtue theory can help us think about these decisions, I start with the work of Rosalind McDougall. In "Parental Virtue: A New Way of Thinking about the Morality of Reproductive Actions," McDougall uses a virtue theory approach to consider reproductive decision making especially in relation to choosing for or against certain traits. Given the parallels between her analysis and ours, her theory is a good starting point. Also, McDougall proposes some initial virtues that may be specific to parenthood. Included in these is the virtue of future-agent focus, which draws on Feinberg's theory. Thus, an analysis of her virtue of future-agent focus will help further clarify the distinction between my approach and the right to an open future approach.

To begin, McDougall adopts the basic virtue theory framework for deciding about moral or immoral actions and applies it to parental actions to come up with this general description of right action:

1. The Criterion of Right *Parental* Action: An action is right if and only if it is what a virtuous parent would do in the circumstances.
2. The Nature of the Virtuous *Parent* Claim: A virtuous parent is one who has and exercises the parental virtues.
3. The Nature of the *Parental* Virtues Claim: *Parental virtues are character traits conducive to the flourishing of the child, taking facts about human reproduction as given.* (Emphasis after colon added. McDougall 2007, 184)

We see from this that parents must exercise parental virtues and parental virtues require parents to cultivate traits that support the child's flourishing. We also see that facts of human existence play a role in helping to decide what traits contribute to flourishing and what we mean by flourishing. I will say more about flourishing as I discuss the parental virtues McDougall introduces.

McDougall proposes three specific parental virtues for consideration—committedness, acceptingness, and future-agent focus. Humans are born dependent and will need care for many years. Based on this fact of human existence, McDougall proposes the virtue of committedness or the idea that parents should be prepared to nurture the child through this period of dependence. Of course, exactly how long of a period this should be is open for debate. I consider this virtue in more depth in chapter 6. The latter two parental virtues seem more applicable to the cases we are considering here so I will focus on them.

Children are also born with a variety of traits related to personality or temperament, talents, likes and dislikes, and so forth. Given the generally unpredictable nature of traits children are born with, McDougall proposes a virtue of acceptingness. In short, parents should be accepting of any trait their child has that is compatible with human flourishing. McDougall acknowledges that the virtue of acceptingness can apply to a wide range of traits—including those related to social acceptance. For example, if you have a child that is quick to anger, McDougall claims the parent does not need to be accepting of this trait and could justifiably work to change it. This is precisely because this trait will make it difficult for the child to get along in life and, in this way, can undermine flourishing. So does this mean parents have a duty to uphold social norms? How far should parents go in promoting social acceptance? I will return to these questions in the later discussion.

Finally, McDougall introduces the virtue of future-agent focus. As she describes it, this virtue is very similar to Joel Feinberg's right to an open future and Deena Davis's modification of that right:

> Recognizing the child as a future moral agent, the good parent acts in particular ways (such as keeping life-possibilities open, and empowering the child with sufficient value structure to enable present and future decision-making). (McDougall 2007, 186)

In sum, we must protect the child's future autonomy by leaving some range of choices open and give the child enough moral education to be able to make these choices for him- or herself. The first thing we should notice is that this is a two part definition: (a) keeping life possibilities open and (b) empowering the child with sufficient value structure to enable present and future decision making.

Feinberg mainly addresses "b" in his section on the paradoxes surrounding a right to an open future—namely, how can we protect a child's right to make future decisions based on her own values and goals when those values and goals will be largely shaped by the parents? Part of the problem for Feinberg is that his theory rests heavily on a conception of autonomy that needs to identify "authentic" desires. In contrast, our understanding of virtue theory highlights a natural progression in the development of moral autonomy.

Recall from chapter 1 that moral development includes teaching children critical discernment. I also proposed that authoritative parenting was likely the best approach for developing these moral skills. What is important here is that the process is meant to help children develop their own skills in moral decision making. In other words we are teaching the child to be a future moral agent. Thus, I believe part "b" of this virtue is primarily fulfilled by the kinds of activities outlined in chapters 1 and 2. If you are training your child to make choices and act in the world, then you will need to let the child practice making choices. In this way, the parent is not only protecting future autonomy, but developing it. The kinds of choices children are allowed to make at any given time will depend on maturity and the potential impact on flourishing.

Which brings us to part "a" of the definition of the virtue of future-agent focus. Instead of relying on Feinberg's theory and the idea of keeping open as many options as possible, I return to the idea of flourishing. If a primary goal of parenting is the flourishing of the child (as McDougall argues it is), then we can approach these decisions by asking how they would impact the child's future flourishing. Unlike Feinberg's maximizing theory, I believe attention to flourishing will help us support Millum's more modest approach—a "reasonable" set of skills and options. To do this we must first say a bit about flourishing.

What Is Flourishing?

Recall from chapter 3 that flourishing is a kind of living well. If we cultivate the development of virtues and live as a virtuous person, this will help us to live a "good life." However, what does it mean to live a good life? As we have said, part of this relates to being a certain kind of person. Being a person of virtuous character leads one to make ethical decisions, but I think Aristotle believes this will also be helpful in more practical ways. We know that, for Aristotle, what counts as a good life should be founded—in some sense—on our human nature. I agree; however, to avoid the baggage associated with a concept like human nature, I prefer something like facts of human existence. To give us one way to think about how flourishing might inform parental decision making, I turn to the work of Michael Bishop as he tries to bring philosophical theories about well-being together with the empirical research produced via positive psychology studies.

Bishop argues for what he calls a "network theory of well-being." The idea is we have various attitudes, traits, and interactions with the world. If these come together in the correct way, they create a self-reinforcing loop that contributes to overall well-being:

> If you were to describe a person with well-being, you would describe a host of objective and subjective facts about the person, including (1) positive feelings, moods, emotions (e.g., joy, contentment), (2) positive attitudes (e.g., optimism, hope, openness to new experiences), (3) positive traits (e.g., friendliness, curiosity, perseverance), and (4) successful interactions with the world (e.g., strong relationships, professional accomplishment, fulfilling hobbies or projects). These elements are nodes in a causal network. Each node is causally connected to some of the other nodes—it fosters some and is fostered by others. The network theory holds that to have well-being is to instantiate a positive causal network or fragments of a positive causal network. (Bishop 2015, 6)

We can see that these positive causal networks (PCNs) are self-reinforcing loops of positive reinforcement and we can have these PCNs in various aspects of our life such as friendships, intimate relationships, and work. For example, you do well on a project at work, get praised by your boss, which motivates you to continue to do your best at work. These can also spill over into other areas. For example, the positive reinforcement you receive at work may boost your confidence, which allows you to finally ask out the guy you like at the gym. If he says yes and the date goes well, you may eventually develop another PCN in the form of an intimate relationship.

Bishop argues that our well-being is connected to the breadth and depth of our PCNs. The more we have (breadth) and the stronger the self-reinforcing loop (depth), the greater our overall well-being. This may sound like a maximizing theory, but I think the "depth" portion can lead to natural restraints on the "breadth" portion. For example, friendships are a common source of PCNs. However, there is a limit to how many friendships you can cultivate at one time—especially intimate friendships that tend to be deeply rewarding. For these reasons, I think Bishop's theory is not maximizing. Instead, he would probably say we need to be able to cultivate PCNs in the "normal" or "major" areas of our life such as family, work or school, friendships, hobbies, or other social groups. Whatever is important to you as an individual, if you can develop PCNs in these areas of your life, it will lead to overall well-being (or a kind of flourishing). I would say the presence of a situation that undermines PCNs is more significant than the absence of a specific PCN. For example, being forced to play a sport you are not good at would lead to the opposite of a PCN. Therefore, we could say that a "reasonable" amount of skills and choices leaves open enough options for a child to develop a variety of PCNs in his or her adult life.

I admit this is still vague, but this may be the best we can do for now. In her work on the action-guiding aspects of virtue theory, Rosalind Hursthouse argues that virtue theory gives us "v-rules"—loose rules connected to the virtues. These would include things like "be kind" or "be honest." However, what it means to fulfill these rules or virtues in any given situation will take some consideration, which is why we need practical wisdom. In this way, the facts of a situation are relevant, but they do not automatically tell us what to do.

> Hence it was recognized that a certain amount of virtue and corresponding moral or practical wisdom (*phronesis*) might be required both to interpret the rules and to determine *which* rule was most appropriately to be applied in a particular case. (Emphasis in original. Hursthouse 2001, 40)

Hursthouse reiterates that other ethical theories have this same problem (as we have seen, a rights-based approach also suffers from indeterminacy). Indeed, she claims that any moral theory that gives a decision procedure simple enough for any clever adolescent to plug in variables and get an answer is not an adequate theory (Hursthouse 2001, 18). Therefore, we need sufficient wisdom to weigh the facts and circumstances in relation to specific virtues and potential actions. In relation to the kinds of decisions we are interested in, this practical wisdom would include both knowledge about your child as well as knowledge about the potential implications of whatever decision is under consideration.

Perhaps more importantly, we should notice how our discussion has shifted the focus. Instead of beginning with a set of rights attached to adults and trying to discover how far we can go in preserving these for children who will one day be adults, we begin with the child. We are presented with a child and then faced with a choice. In considering the scope or limits of this choice, the boundary is not how many rights can we preserve, but what does this child need to flourish now and in the future? The approach I have outlined here gives us some guidance in assessing these decisions. Also, virtue theory has the benefit of being context-dependent. As Millum implies in his critique, these decisions will generally have to be decided on a case-by-case basis. Sometimes the "case" may be a general issue or procedure. Other times the "case" will be a specific family making a specific decision.

Revisiting the Cases

Now let us see what difference this shift in focus makes in analyzing our cases. I start by returning to the virtue of acceptingness. According to McDougall, this virtue requires parents to be accepting of any character trait that is conducive to flourishing. However, flourishing also relates to social acceptance so this virtue leaves us with some difficult questions in relation to our cases—especially intersex and transgender. Many parents agree to intersex surgeries because physicians tell them that the child's gender development requires acceptance by the community and, for the community to give that acceptance, the child's gender should be unambiguous. Similarly, a parent might discourage a transgender child from expressing her chosen gender out of fear the child will be face social ostracism. To address these questions, I return to the discussion of parental wisdom and attentive love introduced in chapter 2.

In *Becoming Nicole*, we follow the story of a family raising a transgender child. Neither the mother, Kelly, nor the father, Wayne, had any previous experience with transgender children or adults. A significant part of the story is the parents' journey to understanding and acceptance, but the different parental responses are informative. Nicole (born Wyatt) presented as a girl from an early age. She gravitated to girly things and actually declared herself to be a girl from the time she was in preschool. Neither parent knew what to make of this or how to handle Nicole's continual demands to present herself as a girl.

Although she would not use this language, Kelly exhibited attentive love in making her decisions. Recall that attentive love is the ability to see the child for who he or she is, not who we want him or her to be. It is also to be attuned to shifts in development and the child's needs. It is a kind of being with and being there for the child. In this case, Kelly could see how strongly Nicole felt about this and—perhaps more importantly—how much it pained Nicole when they refused these demands or someone made her feel embarrassed or ashamed of these desires. Therefore, Kelly tended to allow Nicole to express these aspects of herself as much as possible. Kelly was still influenced by cultural norms that lead her to question her own actions ("Should I allow Nicole to do this? Or am I causing more harm?") and worry for Nicole's safety and, in response to these concerns, she continued to research the situation and seek out resources. In this way, Kelly and Nicole grew together and—as they did—Kelly became more comfortable in her own decisions and better at advocating for Nicole.

In contrast, Wayne had a much more difficult time. Wayne was more committed to cultural norms as well as his own hopes and dreams for what it meant to raise a son.

> Wayne had been on a longer journey than anyone else in the family. He knew it had been Kelly, not he, who had been there for Nicole since day one. Even Jonas [her twin] had always accepted Nicole as his sister, never mourning the loss of a brother the way Wayne mourned the loss of a son. . . . It had taken him years, but he'd slowly come to realize the problem wasn't Nicole, and it certainly wasn't Kelly. He had been the problem all along. (Nutt 2016, 142–43)

Part of what took Wayne so long to come to this realization was that he ignored a key source of parental wisdom—attentive love. His way of coping was to withdraw from the family by devoting long hours to work and hobbies. Thus, it took him much longer to see Nicole/Wyatt for who she really was.

How does this relate to the social acceptance portion of acceptingness? Could this virtue say Wayne's approach was correct because it safeguarded Nicole's acceptance in the community? I think our discussion of attentive love shows why this is not the case. Certainly parents want their children to be able to make friends, have relationships, and participate in a variety of activities. Also, bullying and violent attacks are a real worry for transgender youth. However, these fears need to be balanced against the needs of the child. Suicide is also a real worry for transgender youth. While this is sometimes related to bullying, it can also relate to the inability to be themselves. As Julia Serano explains in her decision to transition from a man to a woman:

> Unlike most forms of sadness that I've experienced, which inevitably ease with time, my gender dissonance only got worse with each passing day. And by the time I made the decision to transition, my gender dissonance had gotten so bad that it completely consumed me; it hurt more than any pain, physical or emotional, that I had ever experienced. . . . When I made the decision to transition, I honestly had no idea what it would be like for me to live as female. The only thing I knew for sure was that pretending to be male was slowly killing me. (Serano 2007, 86)

Similarly, Kelly's decision to support Nicole was mainly in response to the pain Nicole was experiencing. She could tell from Nicole's reactions how important this was for her. Kelly's attentive love helped her see that—in this instance—it was better (more virtuous) to help Nicole find a way to be who she needed to be rather than to make Nicole conform to prevailing gender norms. We can see how the virtue of acceptingness along with open-mindedness and flexibility allowed Kelly to act as a virtuous parent would.

Turning to the case of intersex infants, it is more difficult for parents to use attentive love here. These parents are faced with a newborn and the need to make decisions before they will come to know this child's personality or gender preferences. Instead, these parents are faced with a barrage of advice from medical professionals. In this case, parents will need to draw on other aspects of practical wisdom—mainly, expanding their knowledge about the condition and treatment options. This would include doing some of their own research outside of what the medical professionals tell them. It might also include seeking out adult intersex individuals to gain more experiential knowledge, albeit vicariously. Needless to say, this will be an easier task for some individuals than others. For most parents confronted with an intersex newborn, this will be the first time they have heard of such a thing. Without knowing what the informed consent procedure was like and what resources are available to any specific parents, it is hard to place blame on those who choose in favor of surgery. Parents do the best they can with the information they have.

Before moving on to our third case, let's consider how the case of transgender and intersex would fair in relation to Bishop's PCNs—our proxy measure for flourishing. Again, we could argue that those who conform to social norms will have an easier time developing a variety of PCNs. There is certainly some truth to this. However, Bishop also argues that there is a correlation between self-esteem and PCNs or the idea that the positive benefits of gaining one PCN can lead to the development of other PCNs. It is clear that children who are forced to conform to gender norms that go against their personal gender identity experience various levels of psychological harm. This will inhibit the development of any number of other PCNs. Perhaps more importantly, children who are rejected by their parents for transgender identification or who were subject to cosmetic surgery for intersex experience a disconnect from their own parents. As we will see in the next chapter, a secure attachment to one or more primary caregivers is positively correlated with flourishing. For these reasons, we can see that, in these cases, allowing children to express their chosen gender identity (and supporting them in that choice) will be more conducive to their flourishing (i.e., development of a variety of PCNs).

As we turn to the question of cochlear implants, I will continue to focus on flourishing and the development of PCNs. There are questions related to acceptingness that I will address, but the immediate question of whether to use cochlear implants relates more to the child's ability to flourish. For example, how does the decision to emphasize oral speech or ASL effect the child's ability to develop PCNs? Does rejection of cochlear implants undermine a child's flourishing? When the child is deaf of deaf (that is, a deaf child with deaf parents), the answer seems to be largely no. Deaf parents teach their children ASL and the children readily learn it. There is no gap in learning language and, thus, no gap in cognitive development or communications problems between the parent and child. Also, deaf of deaf children are welcomed into a sub-community that sees itself as a thriving minority. Will the child have fewer options in navigating the hearing world? Possibly. But ours is not a maximizing theory. All we need is a reasonable set of skills and options, or, in the language of flourishing, the ability to develop PCNs in significant areas of a person's life. In this way, being a deaf of deaf child would be more like being born into any relatively insular minority community.

Unfortunately, though, most deaf children are born to hearing parents, which creates a more difficult situation. Like parents who have intersex or transgender children, hearing parents who have a deaf child often have no previous experience with the deaf community. Also, following diagnosis, these parents are immediately confronted with the question of language development and how to best facilitate it. Language development is tied to cognitive development so parents need to ensure that children are exposed to a language they can understand and learn at a very young age. The ability to communicate will affect the parent-child relationship as well.

Unless the parents are going to relinquish the child to deaf parents, the hearing parents will need and want to communicate with their child. Indeed, various kinds of bonding and attachment are necessary for healthy growth of the child, so wanting to be able to communicate with your child—to help facilitate that relationship—is not solely a selfish act. Many parents who give birth to hearing impaired children will try to learn ASL, but this is not always an easy task. Also, depending on where the family lives, their child may have limited access to deaf culture. Presuming the family does not have the resources to move, teaching their child only ASL will have an isolating effect on that child. In this circumstance, giving their child the ability to better navigate the hearing world also gives their child more opportunities for friends and life experiences.

My point here is not to argue that cochlear implants are a miracle cure that makes everything okay for the hearing family with an impaired child. This decision is still a difficult one and hearing parents with a deaf child are forced to make a fraught choice.

> Whereas oral communication places strain upon the deaf member of the family, the decision to sign shifts the power base, placing the greater strain of understanding upon the hearing members. In effect, parents can learn Sign and always speak awkwardly to their child, or they can push their child toward oralism and know that he will always speak awkwardly to them. (Solomon 2012, 93)

As we can see there will still be issues related to communication and a case can be made for dual language training. Given that early language development is so important to early cognitive development and the fact that we cannot always be certain how successful the implant will be, it would seem to be irresponsible to proceed with only oral communication. However, the main point I want to make here is that there are good reasons hearing parents would choose in favor of cochlear implants (despite objections from the deaf community). Some of these reasons relate to the child's future options, but other significant ones relate to the parent-child relationship itself.

In sum, a virtue theory approach helps us see how *both* the deaf parents' use of ASL alone and the hearing parents' decision to use cochlear implants *can be* a moral choice. Both sets of parents are making a decision that will help their children flourish in the environment in which they will grow up. The context-dependent nature of virtue theory emphasizes the pros and cons of both situations, which gives us a more rich understanding of the nature of these decisions. Children who are deaf may have fewer overall options or choices when they are adults but they will be raised in a community where they feel nurtured and accepted. More importantly, the communication necessary for attachment and bonding to primary caregivers will develop naturally as it would in most parent-child relationships. In contrast, deaf children born to hearing parents may have a greater number of options in their life, but will have a more difficult time within their family and community. Regardless of whether the hearing parents opt for implants or emphasize ASL, parent-child communication will be more difficult. These children will also be "different" from the rest of their family and, most likely, the majority of their community. This is not to say that hearing families with deaf children cannot be filled with love and affection. It is merely to highlight the pros and cons of the two situations—many of which are missed in a rights-based analysis.

FINAL THOUGHTS

To conclude, I hope my discussion in this chapter illustrates what a virtue theory approach can add to this debate. Instead of a focus on maximizing autonomy or options, a virtue theory approach turns our attention to other morally salient features that are helpful in constructing a more moderate theory. As a way to further emphasize this shift in focus, I make a parallel with care theory. As Joan Tronto explains, "The moral question of an ethic of care takes as central is not—What, if anything, do I (we) owe to others? But rather—How can I (we) best meet my (our) caring responsibilities?" (Tronto 1993, 137). Similarly, I would say that a virtuous parent does not approach these decisions by trying to figure out how to draw a line between his rights and the child's right to future autonomy. Instead a virtuous parent would approach these decisions with attentive love and a consideration of what might best support the child's future flourishing. Sometimes this may require that the parent foreclose some options in favor of others.

Let us end by returning to the Amish case that illustrated the indeterminacy of a rights-based theory. Again, I think the contextual nature of virtue theory is helpful here. If we return to the theory of PCNs, we can see that it would be possible for children to flourish within or without of the Amish community. Clearly, much of this will relate to their personal temperament and talents. Perhaps what is more vexing about isolated communities like this is the choice they present the child with as he or she grows into adulthood. If it is the case that this particular child's "talents and propensities" are such that she would be better off leaving a sequestered community, then she will also be cutting off another significant source of PCNs. By leaving the community, the child will be breaking ties with her home community of family and friends. Thus, children in these communities must choose between the intimate PCNs they have already established and the potential PCNs they might cultivate in school and work in the larger community. Other children who reject a parents' religion (or even closely held values and beliefs) may face a similar situation, but the more separate the community the more significant this loss is likely to feel.

From this we can see that, while the question of education and opportunities is not insignificant, it is at best only part of the issue. Children are not isolated, autonomous adults. They grow up embedded in a number of intimate and significant relationship and that will affect both the nature of their future choices/decisions and their future flourishing. In this way, the "paradoxes" identified by Feinberg go beyond socialization. There are a variety of relationships (for example, with parents, siblings, grandparents, and friends) that will play a significant role in the child's future options and ability to flourish. Yet, a rights-based theory has little to say about this beyond setting limits on parental decision making.

NOTES

1. For an overview of the kinds of disorders and the development of the approach discussed here, see (Kipnis and Diamond 1999).

2. The discussion here and later in the chapter is significantly influenced by the discussion of hearing parents who have deaf children in Andrew Solomon's *Far from the Tree* (Solomon 2012).

3. However, there are promising treatments being developed that could actually cure hearing loss and, thus, turn a deaf child into a hearing child (correspondent 2017).

Chapter Six

Deciding to Become a Parent

In April of 1997, Tony Randall became a father for the first time at the age of 77. A couple of years later, he became a dad again at the age of 79. In 2004, he died at the age of 84. His daughter Julia Laurette, was 7 years old. His son, Jefferson Salvini, was 5 years old.

In the last year of his residency, Paul Kalanithi was diagnosed with lung cancer. He and his wife stored sperm before he began his first treatment. After some discussion, they decided to proceed with fertility treatments. His wife became pregnant and gave birth to a baby girl. Cady was 8 months old when her father died.

Jack and Diane are in love. They decide to get married and start a family. After some time, Jack decides he does not enjoy being married with kids. He packs his things and leaves the family. His daughter is 6 years old.

In each of these cases, a person takes on the responsibilities of parenthood only to leave while the children are still young. Should we be bothered by these cases? Has this person done something wrong? To sort out how we might think about these parental decisions, I return to Rosalind McDougall's virtue of committedness (introduced in the previous chapter). While I agree with McDougall that this should be considered a parental virtue, I will give different reasons for why—which leads (I think) to different implications for what the virtue entails. I begin the chapter with a general discussion of why we should consider committedness a parental virtue and what I mean by this virtue. After this general introduction, I return to the cases introduced at the beginning of the chapter to flesh out what this means for parents and what they would have to do to live up to such a virtue.

Before getting into the specifics of this discussion, I want to emphasize that this is a moral argument. Even though there may be instances when it is immoral for *some* people to procreate, I do not believe this can be immediately translated into regulations or legal restrictions. In fact, I believe there are practical reasons for *not* legally mandating this moral obligation.[1] Also, when I use the term "parent" I mean the social parent or the person(s) who has taken responsibility for raising a particular child. This may or may not be the biological parent.

COMMITTEDNESS AS A PARENTAL VIRTUE

Let us begin by thinking about why we would even want to call committedness a parental virtue. As we have seen, virtues are tied to flourishing, and our understanding of flourishing should be grounded in facts about human existence. When introducing her theory of parental virtue, Rosalind McDougall argues that the specific virtues we may want to call parental virtues are those character traits that lead to a child's flourishing (McDougall 2007). She also begins to flesh out what we would want to count as parental virtues by considering the facts of human reproduction. Therefore, in order to determine what the virtue of committedness entails, we must consider facts about human reproduction. In this section, I briefly introduce three facts of human reproduction that argue in favor of adopting the virtue of committedness.

Fact #1: Humans are Born Helpless

We are born helpless. As such we require assistance and nurturance for many years. Exactly how many years is debatable depending on when you believe humans reach maturity, but the basic idea is a fact. For McDougall, this fact alone means that parents should be willing and able to nurture their child to adulthood. Although not using a virtue ethics approach, Onora O'Neill makes a similar argument in her discussion of reproductive autonomy.

> An adequate future for children and their long dependence must aim to ensure that each child is born not just to an individual who seeks to express himself or herself, but to persons who can reasonably intend and expect to be present and active for the child across many years.[2] (O'Neill 2002, 62)

As we can see, McDougall and O'Neill seem to believe the fact that children are born dependent and will require emotional and physical support for a number of years supports a virtue of committedness. I disagree. This fact merely requires that anyone choosing to have a child see to it that the child is cared for until maturity. It does not (by itself) require that it be the *same* person who bore the child or even the same person over the course of the child's life.

Assuming I am one of the people responsible for bringing a child into the world, then I certainly have a responsibility to ensure that someone takes care of this vulnerable being. However, I do not believe it is a violation of the virtue of committedness to hand this responsibility over to another capable adult. We will see why when we get to our discussion of the wrong in violating the virtue of committedness. Suffice it to say here that the fact of human dependency merely requires some person meets the child's needs—it does not (on its own) assign responsibility to a specific person. However, I will grant that those who are responsible for bringing the child into existence have a responsibility to see to it that someone takes responsibility for the child.

Fact #2: Children Form Attachments to Primary Caregivers

Children develop attachments to primary caregivers and this is a good thing. In her review of the important aspects of parenting, Susan Golombok argues that "secure attachment relationships are of far-reaching importance for many aspects of psychological well-being in childhood and adult life" (Golombok 2000, xii). She goes on to argue that other factors—such as the child's own personality and the social circumstances the child grows up in—are also important, but attachment to one or more primary caregivers is still of major importance.

Since I am not worried about a utilitarian-type theory, I will not spend much time arguing about potential long-term consequences of losing a caregiver. It is clear that many children can and do live flourishing lives despite the loss of a primary caregiver. For my purposes, we need only to focus on the fact that a strong, secure attachment to one or more primary caregivers will help *facilitate* the child's flourishing. Specifically, it is protective against psychological and behavior problems in childhood and adulthood. Golombok summarizes the general outcomes like so, "Children who become securely attached feel better about themselves, and have better relationships with others, than those who develop insecure attachment relationships" (Golombok 2000, 101). Again, we are discussing general facts of human existence. There may be exceptions to any rule, but, in general, secure attachments promote human flourishing.

For this reason, we now see that the specific caregiver does matter. It is true that the primary caregiver does not have to be the biological parent, but the social parent(s)—whoever the child develops an attachment to—will play a significant role in the child's life. In this way, the role of caregiver is not infinitely interchangeable. Indeed, many would argue, based on the need for secure attachments to a small number of caregivers, the more often this role changes, the worse off the child is.

Fact #3: Relationships Require Time and Attention

To develop a quality relationship requires some undefinable quantity of time. This is the hardest fact to specify, but it does seem to be a fact. If you are too busy or distracted to spend hardly any time with your child, then you are unlikely to develop a good relationship. Children need attention (especially young children). In relation to fact number two, children need to know that you will be available when they need you in times of fear, anxiety, or distress. This is what constitutes a secure attachment relationship. It is hard to do this, if you are not physically present. This is often why mothers are traditionally the primary attachment figure. It is more common for mothers to quit work or restrict their work hours such that they are the primary adult available. In this way, it is not gender that dictates the primary attachment figure so much as who spends time developing the relationship.

I also think this fact shows why committedness is a virtue that is particularly amenable to Aristotle's notion of the Golden Mean. On the one extreme, we have the parent that is always working or busy with some other project. The cultural image is that this parent never has time to play or just be with his or her child. Indeed, this type of parent is often clueless about what sort of person his or her child is and, thus, may actually be estranged from the child once he or she is an adult. On the other extreme, we have the over-controlling parent who is not only constantly present, but also tries to do too much. We actually have a shorthand for this extreme, the "helicopter parent," constantly hovering and constantly intervening to the point that the child never learns the skills needed to be independent and take care of him- or herself. Thus, the virtuous parent needs to apply the doctrine of the mean to this aspect of the virtue of committedness.

Again, I cannot give an exact account of where this mean will lie. As with other examples, it will be specific to the situation. For a further discussion of how to navigate this mean, I refer readers back to chapter 2 and my discussion of practical wisdom and parenthood. What is important for our discussion here is the fact that parenthood is a *relationship*. When one becomes a parent, one is embarking on a relationship with another person. However, unlike other relationships, the child has no say in whether to enter the relationship. The parent will also have the power to set the tone of that relationship. Certainly a specific child's needs and personality will influence the nature of the relationship and, the older the child gets, the more he or she can contribute to how the relationship unfolds. However, it is still the case that the parent decides whether and on what terms to enter into this relationship.[3]

A Virtue Explained

Given that we are adopting a virtue theory approach and the ultimate end of virtue theory is eudaimonia or flourishing, I agree with McDougall that the primary goal of parenting is the child's flourishing. Based on this, she argues that the specific *parental* virtues are those character traits that facilitate the child's flourishing, and flourishing is tied to facts of human existence. Keeping these as general as possible, we see that having a secure, stable attachment to one or more primary caregivers helps facilitate a child's flourishing. For these reasons, I argue that a virtue of committedness is tied to these primary attachment relationships. Thus, it is not the mere biological fact of having a child that entails a virtue of committedness, but the creation of an attachment relationship.

We can make a kind of deductive argument in favor of this virtue by considering both the primary purpose of parenting and the facts previously outlined.

1. Parental virtues should facilitate flourishing for the child.
2. A stable, secure attachment to one or more primary caregivers promotes flourishing in children.
3. A stable, secure attachment requires the primary caregiver be engaged with a child for a number of years.
4. Therefore, committedness (or the ability and desire to be present and care for a child to maturity) is a parental virtue.

When framed this way, we can see the connection to our understanding of virtue theory. We can also see the virtue of committedness has an obvious counterpart—the vice of abandonment.

This argument raises two further questions. The first question is what if a person is strongly committed to something (in this case parenthood), but he is not able to fulfill this commitment. At the time he took on this commitment, he thought he would be able to do it, but it turns out he was wrong. It seems to me we would have to say that this person has violated this virtue, but the blame may be mitigated. Suppose I promise to pick you up from the airport. The time comes to leave for the airport and my car will not start. Instead of going to the airport, I have to call a tow truck. How you respond to this may depend on what you know about me. Is this an anomaly? Is it the case that I am normally a very responsible person and this is just a bit of bad luck? Or, is it the case that I am known for not taking proper care of my car, so I probably should have known better than to make this promise in the first place? In this way, intentions, circumstances, and self-knowledge all matter. Indeed, Aristotle would require us to have some self-reflection about the kind of person we are. It is necessary when making decisions about how to culti-vate the virtues.

Another question we might ask is how strong this commitment needs to be and whether anything can take precedence over it. I would answer this in two ways. First, what it means to live up to this commitment on a day-to-day basis will depend on the child, the parent, and the circumstances. We should all hope to find our golden mean based on the specifics of our life circum-stances. For some guidance on this, I would refer readers back to our discus-sion of practical wisdom in chapter 2. My second response addresses the bigger question of whether there could be other things that might trump this virtue. Again, I think this would depend on the intention and the circum-stances. For example, later in the chapter, I consider the case of a parent who leaves to take a lucrative job away from the family. If this is done in consul-tation with the family and in service to the needs of the family, then I believe it could be a moral option.

To summarize, our three facts of human reproduction or, perhaps more accurately, facts about the nature of childhood and the parent-child bond support McDougall's claim that committednesss should be considered a pa-rental virtue. Children need care for a number of years and having a small number of stable caregivers over this time period gives children a strong foundation for growth and development. However, to reiterate my earlier point, I do not believe this has to be the biological parents. If a person knows she is not up for the task and relinquishes the child before attachment bonds, then it is certainly feasible that another can step in and meet these needs. For these reasons, I do not believe adoption or surrogacy automatically violate the virtue of committedness. As Rosalind Hursthouse points out in her dis-cussion of adoption, these situations may not be ideal, but they do not under-mine the possibility of realizing the goods that can come from parenting. Similarly, I will argue that a key good of parenting (and what makes the virtue of committedness compelling) is the relationship itself, thus, to relin-quish the child before such a relationship develops mitigates the primary wrong in violating the virtue of committedness. Admittedly, in our current society, genetics and family history are often important factors in identity formation so, if a child is denied access to this information, it can be a kind of harm. In this way, adoption and other forms of parenting may be "second best" options (as Hursthouse calls them), but I am still not convinced they are a violation of the virtue of committedness because they avoid what I see as the primary wrong-making nature of the actions that do violate that virtue.

With this basic understanding of the virtue, I return to our initial cases to further explore what this means for parents and what it means to live up to this virtue. This next section focuses mainly on the cases of having a child when you know you are close to death. Much like earlier discussions, I argue that motivations and intentions matter. Children are people, not property and, as such, they deserve respect. You are not buying an object that can be used and discarded on a whim. You are inviting a person into a relationship—and not just any person, but a particularly vulnerable person who will be dependent on you for physical and emotional support. I emphasize the motivations behind these decisions, but also begin to further explain the nature of the relationship that creates a foundation for the virtue of committedness.

As we saw in the last chapter, many approach parental decisions as a question of parental autonomy or rights versus potential harms to the child. I find this approach counterintuitive. I think a closer parallel to this relationship would be relationships between friends. Admittedly, this is not a perfect analogy because friendship relationships are usually between relative equals. Also, when entering a relationship with a friend, I should not have control over whether the other person chooses to enter the relationship. In contrast, children (in normal circumstances) have no choice about whether to enter into this relationship. Still we can consider the norms of friendship as a starting place for thinking about moral and immoral actions in intimate relationships.[4]

After discussing the premature death cases, I return to the case of divorce or separation—or a more willful abandonment of parental responsibilities. I use this case to further explore the wrong in disrupting the secure attachment relationship. Indeed, I think there can be an added layer of harm in *choosing* to terminate this relationship that is not present in the case of death.

THE INTRINSIC GOOD OF PARENTING

Now that we have good reasons for considering committedness a parental virtue, I turn to a discussion of how it could or should figure into parental decision making. Similar to our discussion of body modifications, I wish to avoid the language of rights and autonomy—just because we can do something does not mean we should. As Hursthouse states in her discussion of abortion:

> So whether women have a moral right to terminate their pregnancies is irrelevant within virtue theory, for it is irrelevant to the question "In having an abortion in these circumstances, would the agent be acting virtuously or viciously or neither?" (Hursthouse 1991, 235)

Similarly, the motivating question for this section is "In choosing to have a child in these circumstances, would the agent be acting virtuously or viciously or neither?" To begin to answer this question, I start by returning to our initial cases and the reasons they give for making this choice.

Admittedly, I cannot know all the reasons and considerations that went into these decisions; however, we get some insight into the decision making process from interviews and Kalanithi's book. For Randall, we have his wife's assertion that he "desperately" wanted to have kids (Newman 2008). Similarly, from a public statement, Randall says, "Now imagine the pleasure of a man who wanted children all his life." And, speaking about his son's acting abilities, "I hope Jefferson will become an actor better than his old man. My only sorrow is that I'll never be able to act with him" ("Tony Randall Says It's Never Too Late to Be a Father, from Dadmag.com" n.d.). From these excerpts, Randall's main motivation appears to be a desire to be a parent and the joy kids would bring him in his last years of life.

We have a bit more from Kalanithi's reflections, but not much. In their discussions about whether to have a child, Kalanithi and his wife seem to be primarily focused on their own needs: Would it make the pain of dying worse knowing he was leaving behind a child? Would it be too difficult for his wife to care for him and a young child at the same time? How does she feel about being left to finish raising the child by herself? In relation to the child (before they decide to have her), he only says:

> Years ago, it had occurred to me that Darwin and Nietzsche agreed on one thing: the defining characteristic of the organism is striving. Describing life otherwise was like painting a tiger without stripes. After so many years of living with death, I'd come to understand that the easiest death wasn't necessarily the best. We talked it over. Our families gave their blessing. We decided to have a child. We would carry on living, instead of dying. (Kalanithi and Verghese 2016, 143–44)

While I agree that challenges and strife can be good for a person, I am not convinced this is a meaningful kind of suffering. What lesson or experiential knowledge does a young child learn from the loss of a parent? Perhaps we learn a lesson about enjoying the moment or how to effectively process grief, but the younger the child, the less likely it will be that he or she can fully process this lesson. What about as time goes on? Is it possible that as a child gets older and periodically reflects on her life circumstances she might learn valuable lessons about human frailty or how to console others experiencing a similar kind of grief? Perhaps. People often learn some life lesson from tragedy even if it is just a better ability to empathize with others. Still I would question the motive of a parent who intentionally sets her child up to experience a tragedy with the goal (hope?) she will be able to gain something positive from it.

In both of these accounts we begin to see what troubles me about these cases—there seems to be little consideration of the child's perspective. None of these parents seem to seriously consider the questions: What would it mean for these children to lose their parents at such a young age? What does it mean to invite them into a relationship knowing this will be the end result?

Again, I feel the need to reiterate that I am not doing a utilitarian calculus. In both of these cases, the children have plenty of material and social support. For these reasons the long-term harm is mitigated in many ways. In Kalanithi's case, the daughter is so young, she is likely spared much of the emotional trauma as well. The actual harm and benefits in any particular case is not how I wish to approach this question. Instead, I am concerned with the motivations and reasons that go into these decisions and what that means for a potential virtue of committedness. Are a desire to satisfy a life goal and a hope the child will bring joy to your life sufficient reasons to procreate when you know you will not be able to complete your role as parent?

To answer this question, let us take a step back and think about the "decision" to become a parent in general. I use scare quotes to acknowledge that in many circumstances there is no formal decision. My position on this is similar to Elizabeth Brake's theory of voluntary parenthood. She argues that we accrue the responsibilities and obligations associated with parenthood by voluntarily adopting that role.

> Thus, once someone has chosen not to abort, undergone pre-natal medical care, bought some baby clothes, and taken an infant home, the role of parent has been tacitly accepted. In our society, taking a child home as one's own counts as assuming the role of parent—there is no other way to describe this activity, except as baby-snatching. If abortion is an option, then choosing to continue a pregnancy without making plans for adoption constitutes accepting the role of parent. (Brake 2010, 171)

Once one has voluntarily taken on the social role of parent, then the person is responsible for the obligations that come with it. I agree with Brake that we could read these behaviors as a tacit acceptance of the role of parent. Although, my theory would allow space for relinquishing this role soon after birth (before attachment relationships have formed). Since Brake wants to focus mainly on social parenting and not biological parenting, I believe this caveat is compatible with her theory.

While Brake is primarily interested in assessing how one comes to have moral obligations in relation to parenthood, I would like to take a closer look at how the decision to take on this role is made. I recognize many do not approach this as a formal decision, but many do think about it in general terms and have a general attitude toward the idea of parenting. Even in "normal" circumstances, many of the most compelling reasons to become a parent are selfish, such as wanting to carry on your legacy or wanting the experience of being a parent. For these reasons, we may ask whether it is possible for this decision to be motived by concern for the resulting child. Indeed, in *Better Never to Have Been Born*, David Benatar argues that we can never have children for their own sake. I agree with him on this point.[5] However, even if it is impossible to have a child for his or her own sake, this does not mean there can or should be no consideration of the child's perspective or needs. Surely, there are some moral constraints on procreation based on consideration of the resulting child?

For example, suppose I need to take a drug for one year. This drug is known to be toxic to a developing fetus causing significant birth defects. After this one year, my reason for taking the drug will cease and I will be free to procreate without this risk. It would be utterly irrational and irresponsible for me to choose to become pregnant while on the drug rather than deferring my desire for one year. Thus, despite the generally non-rational nature of the decision to become a parent, our desire to parent can and should be limited by some rational constraints.

Where this rational boundary is ultimately drawn will vary greatly between individuals and circumstances. Certainly, there are many who choose to become parents in situations that others deem irresponsible. I will not pursue a detailed discussion of all those situations or give a clear indication of where I would draw the line. My main point here is simply to show that while decisions about parenthood often contain selfish desires and non-rational motivations, it is still the case that most would agree there are *some* constraints on when that decision is morally acceptable. In my current discussion, I am considering whether it is unreasonably selfish to choose to have a child when you know or have good reason to believe you will not live to see your child to adulthood. For further guidance in trying to answer this question, I turn now to arguments about the morality of abortion proposed by Rosalind Husthouse and Margaret Little. Even though their focus is on the decision to not become a parent, the context of their discussion is useful for our purposes here.

In her discussion of abortion, Hursthouse makes the case that, when presented with a choice, we should be open to becoming a parent. Given that she is considering the morality of abortion, she is mainly referring to when one is pregnant and must decide what to do about this pregnancy. She supports this position by returning to the concept of flourishing and claims that we should be open to becoming a parent because parenthood is an intrinsically worthwhile activity:

> If we are to go on to talk about good human lives, in the context of abortion, we have to bring in our thoughts about the value of love and family life, and our proper emotional development through a natural life cycle. The familiar facts support the view that parenthood in general, and motherhood and childbearing in particular, are intrinsically worthwhile, are among the things that can be correctly thought to be partially constitutive of a flourishing human life. (Hursthouse 1991, 241)

For this reason, Hursthouse believes we should be open to the idea of parenting when the opportunity arises. This does not mean a virtuous person would never choose abortion. She admits there are a variety of legitimate reasons a woman may not be willing to bear and raise a child at this time. Her point is simply that this is a worthwhile activity—one that contributes to the good of a life. As such, we should consider it in relation to other worthwhile activities and the variety of human goods that contribute to our own flourishing.

In relation to our current discussion, we might ask what it is about parenthood that makes it intrinsically valuable. Is it simply being able to call yourself a parent? A kind of checking the experience of procreation off your to do list? Is it the knowledge that your legacy (i.e., genetics, name, memory) will live on? I would argue these are insufficient reasons to call this an intrinsically valuable activity. Indeed, I believe it is the *activity* of parenting that makes it intrinsically valuable. What I mean by this is not the day-to-day responsibilities that are not always enjoyable, but the nature of the relationship between parent and child. This is a unique kind of relationship we do not experience in other areas of our life. To help explain what I mean by this, I turn to Margaret Little's discussion of abortion.

In her analysis, Little separates out two moral questions: When should we be open to entering a relationship? What responsibilities follow from a relationship once it is established? In relation to her second question, Little argues that parenthood as a "thickly normative concept" involves "intertwinement":

> In its paradigmatic form, parenthood is a lived, personal relationship, not just a legal status, one that, in the ideal, involves *a restructuring of psyches, a lived emotional interconnection, and a history of shared experiences*. It is because of that lived intertwinement, indeed, that parents' motivation to sacrifice is so often immediate (why parenthood thickly lived is one of the few sites of genuinely virtuous, as opposed to merely continent, action). (Emphasis added. Little 1999, 306)

Here we begin to see what we might find intrinsically valuable about parenthood. It is the nature of this "intertwinement" that captures the good of parenting. This also explains why so many desire to be parents. In addition to other motives, most parents look forward to the relationship they will have with their child.

I would argue this also helps to explain the virtue of committedness. Recall it is not the mere fact of creating a vulnerable being that requires the virtue of committedness. Instead, I have argued this virtue is tied to the creation of a secure attachment relationship that helps to facilitate the child's flourishing. We see a similar sentiment in Little's discussion of abortion. When choosing whether to continue a pregnancy, we can make a choice about whether to enter into this relationship. However, once a person chooses to enter this relationship, special responsibilities follow from the resulting relationship.

Little goes on to argue there are different kinds of parental responsibilities. There are "weighty deontological obligations" that exist regardless of the nature of the relationship, but there are other responsibilities that arise from the "lived and personal relationship" (Little 1999, 306–7). Little is thinking primarily of bodily obligations such as donating a kidney or a duty to gestate, but we can also apply this reasoning to our earlier discussion. Both Randall and Kalanithi seem to be meeting their deontological obligations. Their children have the material support they need and we have no reason to believe the relationships—while they existed—included any kind of abuse or neglect. *If* there is a failure to live up to parental responsibilities, it would appear to be a breach of the responsibilities that grow out of the lived relationship—namely, creating an attachment (intertwinement) that you *know* will end before it is naturally shifting to a different kind of relationship. As we have seen, this makes it harder for the child to flourish, which goes against the primary purpose of parenting. In contrast, if a parent passes away when the child is grown, it does not mean the adult child will be less sad, but it is a different kind of grief and has different implications for the person's development.

Let us think more about the intrinsically worthwhile nature of the parent-child relationship by turning to Aristotle's discussion of friendship. In Book VIII of the *Nicomachean Ethics*, Aristotle proposes three basic types of friendship: (1) those based on utility or usefulness, (2) those based on pleasure, and (3) those based on mutual good will. The first two kinds of friendship are tenuous and often dissolve easily. The third kind of friendship is the most excellent kind of friendship and is more likely to last for a long time. For Aristotle, the parent-child relationship occupies a kind of ambiguous position. He seems to want to put it in the third category, but it appears to be a unique version of that category. The third category generally applies to equals and Aristotle clearly does not see the parent-child relationship as one of equals. Instead, Aristotle claims that each needs to give the other what is owed. Children are owed nurturing and guidance whereas parents are owed respect. In the following discussion, I am not particularly interested in exploring Aristotle's hierarchical view of the parent-child relationship. Instead, I will focus on what Aristotle seems to consider the "nature" of each kind of friendship.

Recall the main reasons given for Randall and Kalinithi's decision to proceed with parenthood were their desire to be parents and the joy the children brought them in their final years of life. Regarding his daughter, Kalanithi says:

> When you come to one of the many moments in life where you must give an account of yourself, provide a ledger of what you have been, and done, and meant to the world, do not, I pray, discount that you filled a dying man's days

with a sated joy, a joy unknown to me in all my prior years, a joy that does not hunger for more and more but rests, satisfied. In this time, right now, that is an enormous thing. (Kalanithi and Verghese 2016, 199)

Compare the reasons they give for choosing to have children to Aristotle's description of the first two kinds of friendship:

Therefore those who love for the sake of utility love for the sake of what is good for *themselves*, and those who love for the sake of pleasure do so for the sake of what is pleasant to *themselves*, and not in so far as the other is the person loved but in so far as he is useful or pleasant. And thus these friendships are only incidental; for it is not as being the man he is that the loved person is loved, but as providing some good or pleasure. (Emphasis in original. 1156a14–19)

To be clear, I do not believe the bonds in the parent-child relationships we are discussing are merely "incidental." However, I do think *a* primary motivation for choosing to have these children was utility and pleasure. I also think this influences the parent-child relationship.

If we think about the nature of the joy and delight these children bring their parents, we see that a certain kind of reciprocity is necessary. I wonder if Randall and Kalanithi would be as satisfied with their choices if their children had a profound disability—especially one that made reciprocity difficult. I do not mean to disparage disabled children or imply that parents can never love them. Indeed, many parents fiercely love their severely disabled children. However, part of how many parents find meaning in that relationship is by embracing their role as long-term caregiver. They become advocates and defenders for their children. Also many parents do find a kind of reciprocity in these relationships, but discovering this reciprocity and achieving this kind of relationship often takes more time with a severely disabled child. The parents need time to understand the unique nature of this child and how he or she expresses himself or herself in whatever way is possible. Also, the kind of reciprocity will often be very different—it may be more subtle and limited. For many parents of disabled children, this is enough. However, for other parents of disabled children, this is a source of ongoing grief—that the child cannot reciprocate the love and affection the parent feels for them (or at least cannot express that affection in a way the parent can understand) (Solomon 2012). My point here is not to say that Randall and Kalanithi would have rejected or failed to love a disabled child. However, I do think, depending on the nature of the disability, they may have found him or her less of a "delight." If experiencing the reciprocity of the parent-child relationship was one of the joys of your dying years, this would be undercut by a child who could not adequately fulfill this role.

So, if we compare the comments Randall and Kalanithi make about why they wanted to become parents and what they found so meaningful about it, it seems to have much in common with friendships based on utility and pleasure. For comparison, consider what Aristotle says about the third kind of friendship, "Now those who wish well to their friends for their sake are most truly friends; for they do this by reason of their own nature and not incidentally; therefore their friendship lasts as long as they are good—and excellence is an enduring thing" (1156b10–12). Again, this is an imperfect analogy because part of what Aristotle finds so good about this kind of friendship is that it is generally occurs between those who are equally good or excellent (i.e., virtuous). However, if we compare the intent or nature of the feeling in these different types of friendship, we see a clear distinction between the previous kinds of friendship and this one. Here we see desire for the other's good for his or her own sake. Thus, we begin to see what I find troubling about the kinds of cases we are discussing. I have admitted that the decision to become a parent is often motivated by selfish and non-rational desires, but these decisions still need to have some consideration of the child who will be born and what is good for her own sake. I see little wishing the child well for her own sake in the discussions to which we have access. Granted, Randall and Kalanithi make sure the children's basic needs will be met and, barring any other tragic circumstances, the children will have another primary caregiver that will be around until adulthood. Yet, they seem unable or unwilling to meaningfully consider what it means to invite a child into this kind of relationship knowing they will not be around for the normal course of the child's life. They do not ask what their deaths will mean for the children and how that should or should not factor into their decision to proceed.

Thus, based on our current analysis and the information we have access to, it appears that Randall, Kalanithi, and others who make similar choices have violated the virtue of committedness, and I think this is what troubles me about these cases. However, I have a hard time condemning these men or, in the language of virtue ethics, considering them "wicked" or "vicious." Given the intrinsic good of parenting, one can understand the desire. Also, they do seem to embrace the relational nature of parenting in whatever ways they can for as long as they can. Consider these reflections from Randall's wife, Heather: "It's horrible to lose a parent at an early age, but our life is not a tragedy because Tony died. He was a loving husband. And since he couldn't have kids with his first wife, he desperately wanted them—so he was an incredibly loving father" (Newman 2008). For these reasons, this might be considered a more minor violation of the virtue of committedness— akin to not being as generous as you could be when the situation calls for it. I am also a little more forgiving in these kinds of cases because it is never clear exactly how long the relationship will last. The parent is inviting the child into a relationship that is perhaps more precarious than we would normally like, but there is still an element of the unknown here that could (or could not) work in their favor. Neither of these men knew for sure when he would die. If lucky they could have more time with their children than they imagined. Still in the normal course of events, they know they will die before the children reach adulthood. For this reason, I feel compelled to call this a violation of the virtue of committedness, but I think there are other behaviors that constitute more serious violations of this virtue.

REJECTING OR THWARTING THE
INTRINSIC GOOD OF PARENTING

Let us turn now to the third case introduced at the beginning of the paper—abandonment via divorce or separation. Unlike the previous cases, we have no reason to question the motivations involved in deciding to have a kid. For our purposes, we can presume Jack and Diane are in love and desire to have kids for all the normal reasons people in love often make this decision. We can further presume that—at the time of procreation—both Jack and Diane are committed to raising the child. Neither has reason to believe he or she will not be able to be present until the child reaches maturity. Now suppose Jack decides to leave. In doing so, he chooses to leave not only the romantic relationship but the children as well. To be clear, I am not condemning divorce in and of itself. There are many people who manage to work out custody arrangements that allow children to continue to have meaningful relationships with both parents. I am concerned about a parent who not only leaves the house, but also deserts the children in a way that neglects and/or actively rejects the relationship he has made with his child. I want to argue this is a significant violation of the virtue of committedness.

To explain why, I return to Little's discussion of abortion. For Little, once you enter into a parenting relationship, you invite and encourage a kind of intertwinement. I have argued that attachment theory or the secure connection to primary caregivers is one way to think about this intertwinement. Once this relationship is established, there are special responsibilities or duties that come from the lived experience of parenting: "it is also because of the lived intertwinement that the child has legitimate expectations of enormous sacrifice, and why failure to provide such assistance would, absent unusual circumstances, be so problematic—it becomes a betrayal of the relationship itself" (Little 1999, 306). Again, Little is thinking about specific kinds of sacrifice such as donating an organ or a duty to gestate. However, if this lived relationship creates expectations of self-sacrifice related to medical needs, then it surely also creates expectations to continue the relationship.

Paralleling Little's argument, I would argue that choosing to exit the parental relationship once a child has developed a significant attachment to you is a moral wrong—unless you have significantly weighty reasons. Again, to quote Little, "it is a form of abandonment blithely to refuse a sacrifice that would, against a lived relationship, be reasonably expected" (Little 1999, 308). I will not give a comprehensive list of acceptable reasons—I am not even sure such a thing is possible. However, some discussion of reasons will help explain why this is a more significant violation than the cases we were discussing in the previous section.

Building on our previous discussion and Little's emphasis on expectations of self-sacrifice, we can say the more selfish or self-centered the reasons combined with little or no consideration of the child, the less likely they are to be morally acceptable. For example, suppose after seven years of marriage, Jack decides he does not like the responsibility of being a husband and father so he simply packs up and leaves. This would be a clear violation of the moral responsibilities he willingly accepted. However, what about other reasons he might leave? Say he no longer loves Diane or he gets an exciting job offer? Are these legitimate reasons to leave?

Certainly a person should not be compelled to remain in a loveless marriage. Indeed, if the souring of the romantic relationship leads to tension and strife, it can be detrimental to the children for the parents to stay together (Golombok 2000). My argument here is that one has unique responsibilities to any children he or she has chosen to parent that go beyond commitments made in a romantic relationship. For this reason, Jack can leave the marriage, but should do what is necessary to continue to fulfill the virtue of committedness to his children. This may mean not moving too far away so he can continue the relationship he has created.

What about the case of a lucrative job offer that would require Jack to move far away from the family? If he unilaterally decides to take this job and did so primarily for his own benefit, then this would still be a clear violation of the virtue of committedness. As Little points out, the lived relationship of parenthood creates some expectations of self-sacrifice. However, if we change some of the details, his leaving *may* be morally acceptable. Here I am thinking about a family that is struggling financially and agrees to endure the hardship of a (hopefully) temporary long-distance relationship for the sake of financial stability. This situation is different in at least two ways. First, there is a clear consideration of the needs of others and the commitments he has made to them. Second, since this is presumably a joint decision (instead of a unilateral one), the family will likely work to maintain connection and relationships as much as possible. In this later scenario, instead of choosing to leave *despite* the needs of his family, Jack leaves *for* their needs. In contrast, if Jack chooses to leave on his own, he is not only choosing to physically distance himself from his children, but has also already created an emotional breech through the betrayal of the relationship.

In sum, once a person voluntarily accepts the role of parent, he or she is then subject to parental obligations. Here I am arguing that parental obligations include doing one's best to fulfill the virtue of committedness. The lived relationship of parent and child creates attachment bonds that help to facilitate flourishing for the child. While personal circumstances may change and romantic relationships come and go, a person cannot abandon his or her child without sufficiently weighty reasons. Even in such a case, the person will have failed to fulfill the virtue of committedness, but sometimes one moral obligation outweighs another or circumstances beyond our control may make it impossible to fulfill our moral obligations.

In the previous section, I argued that failing to fulfill the virtue of committedness due to death was a lesser violation than willful abandonment. While I do believe abandonment is generally a greater violation, reasons and intentions still make a difference. If the violation is prompted by other needs of the family (including the needs of the children), it will be a lesser violation than choosing to leave for selfish reasons. While I do not have the space to fully pursue every option, I can imagine there are other scenarios that would also lessen the violation such as needing to take care of an aging parent or military deployment.

Before leaving this section, I would like to deal with what is perhaps the worst violation of the virtue of committedness. I am thinking about situations where one parent uses divorce as a way to intentionally sever the other parent's relationship with the child.[6] For example, too many of us know situations where a parent fights for sole custody not because he thinks it is best for the children, but because he wants to punish his former lover. In these situations, the one parent is punishing the child in order to punish the other parent. I am more ready to call this kind of behavior wicked and vicious. A parent who chooses to do this not only refuses to consider the good of the child for her own sake, but is also *actively keeping another person from being virtuous.* The parent who severs this relationship denies the other parent the opportunity to fulfill the virtue of committedness.

Also, when thinking about custody and visitation, my theory may have further implications. In her discussion of voluntary parenthood, Brake argues that her approach opens up the possibility of non-traditional parenting relationships. Similarly, the virtue of committedness may require us to rethink moral obligations in relation to children when considering custody and visitation arrangements. For example, a stepparent who has lived with a child for many years such that he has developed a significant relationship with this child would then have moral obligations to the child. While my argument is focused mainly on the parenting relationship, this may also have implications for other significant attachments the child makes with say grandparents, godparents, and special aunts or uncles.

SOME FINAL THOUGHTS

I have argued that the virtue of committedness grows out of attachment bonds formed in the parent-child relationship. I have further argued that choosing to have a child when you know or have good reason to believe you will die before the child reaches maturity and abandoning a child through separation or divorce are both instances that violate the virtue of committedness. However, I believe abandonment is usually a greater violation than death. We see this by considering the choices involved.

While I have expressed some concerns about the motivations involved in the decision to have a child when facing death, I believe the personal circumstances also matter here. For example, how much of a role did previous choices or actions contribute to putting one in this situation? In Kalanithi's case, he had a life plan that included starting a family within a reasonable amount of time. Unfortunately, his plans were thwarted by circumstances beyond his control. In this kind of case, we can see why a person would have a difficult time giving up the desire to be a parent. The intrinsic goods of parenting were part of his life plans and he was working toward that goal. In contrast, Randall claims he "desperately" wanted to be a parent, but does not appear to have done what he could have to make that happen. We are told it was "not possible" with his previous wife. Why? Even if they had issues with infertility, they certainly had the resources to try and work around this or pursue adoption. If it is the case that Randall's wife simply did not want kids, then he still made a choice to forgo this desire in order to stay with her. For these reasons, Randall seems to bear more responsibility for being in a position where he chooses to have kids very late in life. I say "seems" because I do not know the details of his life that influenced his decisions and actions. My main goal here is not to condemn Randall, but to point out that previous choices and decisions can influence moral blameworthiness even in cases of premature death.

Reviewing intentions and actions also shows why cases of abandonment are more likely to present a flagrant disregard for the virtue of committedness. In more circumstances than I can count, people embark on the project of parenthood only to abandon it later. I would argue that this should count as a more "vicious" action under virtue theory because you are walking away from commitments you willingly made. Or, in the worst-case scenario, you are actively working to keep another from fulfilling this virtue. Although I will not pursue it here, I believe this also is more likely to undermine a child's flourishing. It is one thing to know your parent is not around because he died. It is another to know he is still out and about in the world, but simply chose to walk away from you. To use Little's language, this is a clear betrayal of the relationship.

People often consider the decision to become a parent a weighty one. From the discussion here, we can see why this would be the case. Choosing to become a parent is the beginning of a significant relationship. You are inviting a vulnerable person to join you in a relationship that will help shape the future of that child's life. As such, you have made a commitment to this person—one that should not be taken lightly.

NOTES

1. For example, while my moral argument applies equally to men and women, it would be difficult to equally enforce a law against elderly parenthood for both men and women. There would be no easy way to keep men from procreating whereas it would be fairly easy to keep post-menopausal women from procreating.

2. McDougall also uses O'Neill to help explain her understanding of committedness as a parental virtue. Even though I used a longer and slightly different quote than the one McDougall uses, it captures the same sentiment.

3. There is one caveat to this—the parent could be presented with a child radically different than the one he expected to have (see chapter 5). However, it is still the parent who opens himself to this potentiality in choosing to have a child. Also, parents will have the choice to relinquish a child after birth. In contrast, children cannot sever themselves from their parents until they are much older.

4. I use similar analogies in my discussion of trustworthiness in chapter 4.

5. This is not to say I agree with his argument against procreation based on the claim that existence is always a harm. While I do not have the space to give a full refutation to Benatar's position, it would likely be a kind of teleological one. Survival is a basic instinct of any species, so I find any theory that argues for our extinction counterintuitive. Similarly, I do think there are intrinsic goods of living that go beyond his analysis of harm. For these reasons, I would disagree with his overall argument.

6. We could also include cases where one parent "kidnaps" the children—that is the parent takes the children and leaves the country such that it is difficult or impossible for the other parent to have access to them.

Bibliography

Annas, Julia. 1993. *The Morality of Happiness*. New York: Oxford University Press.

Aristotle, and Jonathan Barnes. 1984. *The Complete Works of Aristotle: The Revised Oxford Translation*. Bollingen Series, 71:2. Princeton, N.J: Princeton University Press.

Bartholet, Elizabeth. 1993. *Family Bonds: Adoption and the Politics of Parenting*. Book, Whole. Boston: Houghton Mifflin Company.

Bartky, Sandra Lee. 1990. *Femininity and Domination: Studies in the Phenomenology of Oppression*. New York: Routledge.

Benkov, Laura. 1994. *Reinventing the Family: The Emerging Story of Lesbian and Gay Parents*. New York: Crown Publishers.

Benson, Paul. 1987. "Freedom and Value." *The Journal of Philosophy* 84 (9): 465–86.

———. 1994. "Free Agency and Self-Worth." *Journal of Philosophy* 91 (12): 650–68.

Bishop, Michael. 2015. *The Good Life: Unifying the Philosophy and Psychology of Well-Being*. New York: Oxford University Press.

Bloom, Paul. 2013. *Just Babies: The Origins of Good and Evil*. First Edition. New York: Crown Publishers.

Bok, Sissela. 1999. *Lying: Moral Choice in Public and Private Life*. New York: Vintage Books.

Brake, Elizabeth. 2010. "Willing Parents: A Voluntarist Accounts of Parental Role Obligations." In *Procreation and Parenthood: The Ethics of Bearing and Rearing Children*, 151–77. Oxford, England: Clarendon Press; Oxford University Press.

Brown, Stacia. 2014. "When Parenting Feels Like a Fool's Errand," 2014. http://stacial-brown.com/2014/08/10/when-parenting-feels-like-a-fools-errand-on-the-death-of-michael-brown/.

Burnyeat, M. F. 1981. "Aristotle on Learning to Be Good." In *Essays on Aristotle's Ethics*. Berkeley: University of California Press.

Cannon, Katie Geneva. 1995. *Katie's Canon: Womanism and the Soul of the Black Community*. New York: Continuum.

Coates, Ta-Nehisi. 2015. *Between the World and Me*. First edition. New York: Spiegel & Grau.

Collins, Patricia Hill. 2000. *Black Feminist Thought: Knowledge, Consciousness, and the Politics of Empowerment*. 10th Anniversary. New York: Routledge.

Cross, Katherine. 2014. "The Price of Our Blood: Why Ferguson Is a Reproductive Justice Issue," 2014. http://rhrealitycheck.org/article/2014/08/26/price-blood-ferguson-reproductive-justice-issue/.

Curzer, Howard J. 2002. "Aristotle's Painful Path to Virtue." *Journal of the History of Philosophy* 40 (2): 141–62.

Daar, Judith, Jean Benward, Lee Collins, Owen Davis, Joseph Davis, Leslie Francis, Elena Gates, et al. 2018. "Informing Offspring of Their Conception by Gamete or Embryo Donation: An Ethics Committee Opinion." *Fertility and Sterility* 109 (4): 601–5. https://doi.org/10.1016/j.fertnstert.2018.01.001.

Damasio, Antonio. 2000. *The Feeling of What Happens: Body and Emotion in the Making of Consciousness.* 1st Harvest ed. New York: Harcourt Inc.

———. 2005. *Descartes' Error: Emotion, Reason, and the Human Brain.* New York: Penguin.

Daniels, Ken. 2007. "Donor Gametes: Anonymous or Identified?" *Best Practice & Research Clinical Obstetrics and Gynaecology* 21 (1): 113–28.

Darwall, Stephen. 2002. *Welfare and Rational Care.* Princeton: Princeton Univ Pr.

Davis, Dena S. 1997a. "Genetic Dilemmas and the Child's Right to an Open Future." *Hastings Center Report* 27 (2): 7–15.

———. 1997b. "The Child's Right to an Open Future: Yoder and Beyond." *Capital University Law Review* 26: 93–106.

Devlin, Hannah. 2017. "Breakthrough for Genetic Hearing Loss as Gene Editing Prevents Deafness in Mice." *The Guardian*, December 20, 2017, sec. Science. www.theguardian.com/science/2017/dec/20/breakthrough-for-genetic-hearing-loss-as-gene-editing-prevents-deafness-in-mice.

DiAngelo, Robin. 2011. "White Fragility." *The International Journal of Critical Pedagogy* 3 (3): 54–70.

Dill, Bonnie Thornton. 1988. "Our Mother's Grief: Racial Ethnic Women and the Maintenance of Family." *Journal of Family History* 13 (4): 415–31.

Feinberg, Joel. 1992. *Freedom and Fulfillment: Philosophical Essays.* Princeton, N.J: Princeton University Press.

Firth, Lucy. 2001. "Gamete Donation and Anonymity: The Ethical and Legal Debate." *Human Reproduction* 16 (5): 818–24.

Frye, Marilyn. 1983. *The Politics of Reality: Essays in Feminist Theory.* Trumansburg, N.Y.: Crossing Press.

———. 1992. *Willful Virgin : Essays in Feminism, 1976-1992.* Freedom, Calif.: Crossing Press.

Gardiner, Stephen M., ed. 2005. "Virtue Ethics and Human Development." In *Virtue Ethics Old and New*, 142–58. Ithaca, N.Y.: Cornell University Press.

Gibbs, John C. 2003. *Moral Development and Reality: Beyond the Theories of Kohlberg and Hoffman.* Thousand Oaks, Calif.: SAGE Publications.

Golombok, Susan. 2000. *Parenting: What Really Counts?* Philadelphia: Routledge.

Gropnik, Alison, Ph.D., Andrew N. Meltzoff Ph.D., and Patricia K. Kuhl Ph.D. 1999. *The Scientist in the Crib: Minds, Brains, and How Children Learn.* New York: William Morrow and Company, Inc.

Hale, Janice. 1980. "The Black Woman and Child Rearing." In *The Black Woman*, edited by La Frances Rodgers-Rose, 79–88. Newbury Park, Calif.: SAGE Publications.

Happy. [Electronic Resource (Video)]. 2012. New York, N.Y.: Films Media Group, [2013], c2012.

Harvey, Jennifer. 2018. *Raising White Kids: Bringing up Children in a Racially Unjust America.* Nashville, Tenn.: Abingdon Press.

Helms, Janet E. 2000. *Race Is a Nice Thing to Have: A Guide to Being a White Person or Understanding the White Persons in Your Life.* Topeka, Kans.: Content Communcations.

hooks, bell. 1995. *Killing Rage: Ending Racism.* 1st ed. New York: H. Holt and Co.

Hursthouse, Rosalind. 1991. "Virtue Theory and Abortion." *Philosophy & Public Affairs* 20 (3): 223–46.

———. 2001. *On Virtue Ethics.* Oxford: Oxford University Press.

———. 2006. "Practical Wisdom: A Mundane Account." *Proceedings of the Aristotelian Society* 106 (Journal Article): 285–309.

"Intersex Society of North America / A World Free of Shame, Secrecy, and Unwanted Genital Surgery." n.d. Accessed May 2, 2018. www.isna.org/.

Kalanithi, Paul, and A. Verghese. 2016. *When Breath Becomes Air.* First edition. New York: Random House.

Kerr, Jeannie. 2011. "Habituation: A Method for Cultivating Starting Points in the Ethical Life." *Journal of Philosophy of Education* 45 (4): 643–55.

King, Shaun. 2017. "Jordan Edwards' Family Consumed by Terror, Grief after Police Kill 15-Year-Old Boy." *New York Daily News*, May 4, 2017. Accessed May 9, 2018. www.nydailynews.com/news/national/king-jordan-edwards-family-stricken-terror-boy-death-article-1.3137284.

Kipnis, Kenneth, and Milton Diamond. 1999. "Pediatric Ethics and the Surgical Assignment of Sex." In *Intersex in the Age of Ethics*, edited by Alice Domurat Dreger, 174–93. Hagerstown, Md.: University Publishing Group.

Kittay, Eva Feder. 1999. *Love's Labor: Essays on Women, Equality, and Dependency*. New York: Routledge.

Kraus, Michael W., Paul K. Piff, and Dacher Keltner. 2011. "Social Class as Culture: The Convergence of Resources and Rank in the Social Realm." *Current Directions in Psychological Science* 20 (4): 246–50.

Lareau, Annette. 2003. *Unequal Childhoods: Class, Race, and Family Life*. Berkeley: University of California Press.

Little, Margaret Olivia. 1999. "Abortion, Intimacy, and the Duty to Gestate." *Ethical Theory and Moral Practice* 2 (3): 295–312.

Lorbach, Caroline. 2003. *Experiences of Donor Conception: Parents, Offspring and Donors through the Years*. Philadelphia, Pa.: Jessica Kingsley Publishers.

Lorde, Audre. 1984. *Sister Outsider: Essays and Speeches by Audre Lorde*. Freedom, Calif.: The Crossing Press.

McDougall, Rosalind. 2007. "Parental Virtue: A New Way of Thinking about the Morality of Reproductive Actions." *Bioethics* 21 (4): 181–90.

McGee, Glenn, Sarah-Vaughan Brakman, and Andrea D. Gurmankin. 2001. "Gamete Donation and Anonymity: Disclosure to Children Conceived with Donor Gametes Should Not Be Optional." *Human Reproduction* 16 (10): 2033–38.

Mendell, Patricia, and Jean Benward. 2009. "Talking with Children about Ovum Donation," 2009. Last accessed November 30, 2018. https://www.donorconcierge.com/blog/talking-with-children-about-ovum-donation-2009-afa.

Mills, Charles W. 1997. *The Racial Contract*. Ithaca: Cornell University Press.

Millum, Joseph. 2014. "The Foundation of the Child's Right to an Open Future." *Journal of Social Philosophy* 45 (4): 522–38.

Mueller, Monica. 2013. *Contrary to Thoughtlessness: Rethinking Practical Wisdom*. Lanham, Md.: Lexington Books.

Newman, Judith. 2008. "She Was a 20-Year-Old Intern, He Was 50 Years Her Senior." Marie Claire. January 29, 2008. Last accessed November 30, 2018. https://www.marieclaire.com/sex-love/relationship-issues/tony-randall-wife.

Nutt, Amy Ellis. 2016. *Becoming Nicole: The Transformation of an American Family*. New York: Random House.

O'Neill, Onora. 2002. *Autonomy and Trust in Bioethics*. Cambridge; New York: Cambridge University Press.

Piff, Paul K., Michael W. Kraus, Stéphane Côté, Bonnie Hayden Cheng, and Dacher Keltner. 2010. "Having Less, Giving More: The Influence of Social Class on Prosocial Behavior." *Journal of Personality and Social Psychology* 99: 771–84.

"Position Statement on Cochlear Implants." 2015. National Association of the Deaf. March 7, 2015. https://www.nad.org/about-us/position-statements/position-statement-on-cochlear-implants/.

Potter, Nancy Nyquist. 2002. *How Can I Be Trusted? A Virtue Theory of Trustworthiness*. Lanham, Md.: Rowman & Littlefield.

Ruddick, Sara. 1989. *Maternal Thinking: Toward a Politics of Peace*. Boston: Beacon Press.

Russell, Daniel. 2005. "Aristotle on the Moral Relevance of Self-Respect." In *Virtue Ethics, Old and New*, edited by Stephen M. Gardiner, 101–24. Ithaca, N.Y.: Cornell University Press.

Senior, Jennifer. 2014. *All Joy and No Fun: The Paradox of Modern Parenthood*. New York: Harper Collins Publishers.

Serano, Julia. 2007. *Whipping Girl: A Transsexual Woman on Sexism and the Scapegoating of Femininity*. Emeryville, Calif.: Seal Press.

Sherman, Nancy. 1989. *The Fabric of Character: Aristotle's Theory of Virtue*. Oxford: Clarendon Press.

Solomon, Andrew. 2012. *Far from the Tree: Parents, Children and the Search for Identity*. 1st Scribner hardcover ed. New York: Scribner.

Solomon, Andrew. 2008. Published May 25, 2008. "The Autism Rights Movement." NYMag.Com. Accessed May 1, 2018. http://nymag.com/news/features/47225/.

Stern, Ken. 2013. "Why the Rich Don't Give to Charity." *The Atlantic*, April 2013. https://www.theatlantic.com/magazine/archive/2013/04/why-the-rich-dont-give/309254/.

Steutel, Jan, and Ben Spiecker. 2004. "Cultivating Sentimental Dispositions through Aristotelian Habituation." *Journal of Philosophy of Education* 38 (4): 531–49.

Swartwood, Jason D. 2013. "Wisdom as an Expert Skill." *Ethical Theory and Moral Practice: An International Forum* 16 (3): 511–28.

Tatum, Beverly Daniel. 1997. *"Why Are All the Black Kids Sitting Together in the Cafeteria?" And Other Conversations about Race*. 1st ed. New York: BasicBooks.

Taylor, Paul C. 2003. *Race: A Philosophical Introduction*. Cambridge: Polity Press.

Tessman, Lisa. 2005. *Burdened Virtues: Virtue Ethics for Liberatory Struggles*. New York: Oxford University Press.

Thorpe, J. R. 2017. "To Guys Who Think It's 'Hard To Be A Man' Right Now, I've Got Some News For You." *Bustle*. Accessed May 7, 2018. https://www.bustle.com/p/to-guys-who-think-its-hard-to-be-a-man-right-now-ive-got-some-news-for-you-3344482.

"Tony Randall Says It's Never Too Late to Be a Father, from Dadmag.Com." n.d. Accessed April 20, 2018. www.dadmag.com/tonyrandall.php.

Tronto, Joan C. 1993. *Moral Boundaries: A Political Argument for an Ethic of Care*. New York: Routledge.

Valian, Virginia. 1998. *Why so Slow? The Advancement of Women*. Cambridge, Mass: MIT Press.

Walker, Lawrence J., and Karl H. Hennig. 1999. "Parenting Style and the Development of Moral Reasoning." *Journal of Moral Education* 28 (3): 359–74.

"What Your Baby Knows about You." 2010. *Parenting*. December 19, 2010. https://www.parenting.com/article/what-your-baby-knows-about-you.

Winfrey Harris, Tamara. 2015. *The Sisters Are Alright Changing the Broken Narrative of Black Women in America*. Oakland, Calif.: Berrett-Koehler Publishers.

Young, Iris Marion. 1990. *Justice and the Politics of Difference*. Book, Whole. Princeton, N.J.: Princeton University Press.

Index

About the Author

Sonya Charles is an associate professor at Cleveland State University in the Department of Philosophy and Comparative Religion. Her research areas include bioethics (with an emphasis on reproductive ethics), feminist philosophy, autonomy theory, and virtue theory. Most recently, she has published work on nurses and patient autonomy, decision making during childbirth, and using virtue theory to think about the ethics of parenthood.

Made in the USA
Las Vegas, NV
08 January 2024

84096697R00090